KATHY W

The Millennium Candidate

How to Realize
Your True Potential
in the New World
of Work

ELEMENT

Shaftesbury, Dorset · Boston, Massachusetts · Melbourne, Victoria

© Element Books Limited 1999
Text © Kathy Wilson 1999

First published in the UK in 1999 by
Element Books Limited
Shaftesbury, Dorset SP7 8BP

Published in the USA in 1999 by
Element Books, Inc.
160 North Washington Street, Boston, MA 02114

Published in Australia in 1999 by
Element Books and distributed
by Penguin Australia Limited
487 Maroondah Highway, Ringwood, Victoria 3134

Cover design and imaging by Slatter-Anderson
Design by Dale Tomlinson
Typeset by Bournemouth Colour Press, Parkstone
Printed and bound in Great Britain by Biddles Ltd, Guildford & King's Lynn

British Library Cataloguing in Publication data available

Library of Congress Cataloging in Publication data available

ISBN 1 86204 380 9

Contents

PART THREE · **Making it Happen**

The Millennium

Candidate

is a new, dynamic

breed of professional

who will have

the nerve, stamina

and knowledge

to ride the career

roller-coaster of

the 21st century

Acknowledgements

My deepest thanks to all my clients, students and business associates whose experiences inspired this book.

For the information on Australia, I am indebted to Paul Stevens, Director of the Centre for Worklife Counselling and Elizabeth Mountain, Director of the Youth Bureau Career Information Section at the Australian Department of Employment Education, Training and Youth Affairs.

Thanks also to Jonathan Hinde, Press Officer at the Transcendental Meditation Centre in London.

Foreword

I walked back into the training room and the atmosphere was electric.

I'd left the group alone for ten minutes so they could get acquainted with each other, and already they were engaged in animated discussion and exchanging ideas about how they could re-invest in themselves and fast-forward their careers.

The accountant was sharing his experiences with the teacher, the managing director was listening attentively to the IT professional, and the administrator was sharing a joke with the civil servant. Could these be the same people who, only an hour ago, had joined my Professional Development Course as total strangers?

But that's how it happened. That's how it always happens. We had only just started, but now I knew they would find what they were looking for. As soon as people focus and connect with each other, a whole new world of opportunities opens up for them.

The same goes for you. In the pages of this book, you are going to meet a great many people, people whose experiences will help you to advance your career or find the job that's right for you. Welcome to the Millennium Masterclass.

Introduction

Global recession, economic meltdown, staff shakeouts; even in times of prosperity, we are constantly assailed by fresh horror stories of worldwide financial turbulence and the threat it poses to our lives and jobs. Moreover, there is every sign that this uncertainty and the fear it creates will continue well into the millennium.

As a Career and Stress Management Consultant, I have seen first-hand many casualties of this brave new world, and over the years have helped hundreds of people who have found themselves out of work or struggling to cope in a 'restructured' organization.

The good news is that time and again I have witnessed individuals triumph over setbacks and go on to carve out rewarding careers, whether in an existing job or with a different organization. Whatever their profession, ability or disability, the turning point always comes when they are prepared to let go of limiting beliefs and open themselves up to new ideas. This is equally true of people who are considering their career options for the first time.

Organizations use my services because forward planning is part of their culture, and anticipating change makes good business sense. Individuals also consult me when they face transitions, but many wait until they have reached a crisis point. This means that they have to spend precious time rebuilding their self-esteem before moving on to achieving specific goals. A common refrain is 'If only I had come to you months (even years) ago!' My response is to write this book to help you to plan ahead *from a position of strength*, rather than waiting for events to force your hand.

If you want to succeed in the new world of work, this book is for you. Whether you are currently employed, unemployed or pre-employed, it can help you. My clients come from a range of backgrounds and professions, from graduates to directors. They include:

➠ Workers who have been made redundant
➠ People looking at job options for the first time
➠ Individuals considering self-employment
➠ Staff seeking promotion or a pay rise
➠ Parents returning to work after raising children.

Whatever your background, you need to know that today's employment market is changing, and that tomorrow's employers are looking for a new type of candidate: the Millennium Candidate. The Millennium Candidate is a new, dynamic breed of professional who will have the nerve, stamina and knowledge to ride the career roller-coaster of the 21st century.

From now on, most of us will remain as 'candidates' throughout our working lives; candidates not just for jobs and promotions, but for redundancy, self-employment and a host of new ways of working. You have the potential to become a Millennium Candidate. The secret is to anticipate change and be ready to re-invent yourself as and when necessary.

This book has been designed as a series of interactive training sessions, similar to the ones I use with my clients. Think of yourself as going on a journey into the 21st century, a journey that will require a firm commitment and careful planning. My role is to provide the signposts, but the final destination is for you to decide upon.

In Part One, Meeting the Millennium Challenge, you will learn how to build a personal power base that will act as the platform for all your future efforts, whether you are looking for promotion at work, considering your options or actively engaged in job search. Part Two, The Millennium Campaign Plan, is a practical guide to managing your own career, making vocational choices and mounting an effective job search campaign. Last, but not least, in Part Three, Making it Happen, we will explore ways to stay motivated and maintain peak performance.

Given the accelerated pace of change these days, no book can ever be completely up-to-date where specific professions are concerned. My emphasis, therefore, is on helping you to develop a fresh and innovative approach to work in the millennium by learning how to predict trends and exploit opportunities for yourself. However, throughout the book, and in the appendices, you will find pointers to other publications and sources of information, including the wealth of regularly updated careers and job search sites on the Internet.

Ideally, when first planning a new career, you should seek the services of an adviser, who should have access to systems and documentation that reflect the new opportunities and training options arising each year. He or she can also help you to make sense of the sometimes bewildering amount of data now available on the subject, particularly where the Internet is concerned. Depending on your situation, you can find an adviser or consultant in the private sector or at government centres. Students should make the most of college or university facilities.

In the meantime, to get the best out of this book, go through each chapter in sequence, even if you are in a hurry to get started on job searching. If you really don't have time to do all the exercises, at least read the text. This will ensure that you make the most productive use of the comprehensive job search strategies outlined in Part Two. Rather than leaving everything to the day before the interview, how much better to draw on a compelling body of established knowledge about what motivates employers, together with an equally strong insight into how you match their requirements? The pay-off will be a dramatic improvement in your credibility.

As we journey into the new millennium, we must be ready to

navigate uncharted waters and prepare to live with instability and constant change. However, a relatively small investment of time now will help you to stay on course for the rest of your career, no matter what dramas occur on the global stage.

Successfully managing change always requires a degree of commitment, but remember your whole future is at stake here; do you really want to settle for second best? Rest assured that executives and other senior people would not shrink from the prospect. They regularly set aside significant periods of time for self-improvement (and pay top rates for the privilege).

To bring the training alive, throughout the book I have used brief references to the real-life experiences of my clients and associates, although the names have been changed to preserve confidentiality. To aid revision, you will also find a summary of learning points at the end of each chapter.

Finally, I would never expect my clients to accept what I say on trust, and the same applies to you. My guidance will only be of value if you take the trouble to evaluate it in the light of your own experience. To help you do this, I have included a series of self-assessment exercises.

Part One

Meeting the Millennium Challenge

Chapter One

A New Way of Working

The real revolution in the world of
work will be driven by individuals
who have learned to balance the
profusion of external information
with the wealth of liberating
knowledge within.

Becoming Your Own Knowledge Manager

At first glance, life in the millennium presents a frightening picture, certainly where job prospects are concerned. However, if
you keep your head and make the effort to stay abreast of developments, there is no need to be apprehensive.

On the contrary, the very word 'millennium' is a powerful
symbol of renewal, with enormous potential to focus your career
plans. As we enter the new century, people are being galvanized
into action all around the world, and a great deal of energy is
being mobilized to ensure that it marks a meaningful turning
point in our lives. We can all capitalize on this new vitality and
make it work to our advantage.

Let's start by looking at the new world of work in more detail.
We have already seen radical changes in the labour market as
organisations globalize their operations, restructure themselves
and introduce increasingly innovative technology. The pace of
change is likely to accelerate even further in the future, resulting
in ever more fragmented and mobile working patterns for all of
us. The days of finding a job for life and training for promotion in
the expectation of a secure pension are in decline.

The question, then, is how to prosper in this volatile and

seemingly alien environment? The answer is very straightforward. As the competition for the good jobs and contracts hots up, success will go to those who are able to stand out from the crowd. This means you will have to make yourself *valuable* to the decision makers, and value comes from knowledge.

We live in the age of information, and everywhere we are awash with junk mail, electronic communications, advertisements and media reports. *Information* is what we are told, but it is not the same as *knowledge*. In excess it leads to stress and saps our resources. Knowledge is what we have understood, evaluated and can put to profitable use. Highly marketable and energizing, it represents the central ingredient for career prosperity in the future.

The importance of harnessing expertise has not been lost on companies, which accounts for the popularity of knowledge management systems and the growth of 'knowledge managers'. Organizations realize that to remain competitive they must maintain a strong grip on their 'intellectual' capital by systematically recording and utilizing the diversity of competence at their disposal. This is not just another corporate fad, but something that has a direct effect on the bottom line. The same goes for the individual; if you want to stay ahead of the game, you must become your own 'knowledge manager'.

As you have probably noticed by now, in signing up to become a Millennium Candidate, you have entered the world of marketing. The 'product' you will be promoting is yourself, or more accurately, a mix of your talent and personal qualities. Be aware, too, that you will face fierce competition for the best openings, so a structured campaign plan is absolutely vital. This book is the starting point of your campaign. In its pages you will learn how to:

⇒ interpret labour market trends
⇒ beat stress and limber up physically
⇒ achieve more by doing less
⇒ understand what employers want from you

- think like an entrepreneur
- develop career resilience
- become a lifelong learner
- network for success

Change in the Workplace

Step one in your campaign is to understand how global events affect your career prospects. Although full-time, seemingly permanent jobs have not entirely disappeared, their chances of survival are slim. Few organizations these days can claim immunity from the effects of stock market collapses and merger mania.

As we advance through the 21st century, governments and employers around the world will continue to react to the revolutionary forces affecting labour markets. Exact forecasts for the future are impossible, but the key drivers of change are likely to remain the same for some time to come. They are:

New technology, which has automated many labour intensive processes and improved communications, creating new types of companies and occupations. This also accounts for the increase in mobile workers and 'hot deskers', people who make the most of laptop computers, modems and other electronic gadgetry to eliminate the need for fixed office space. On a global level, billions are moved electronically between countries every day, putting a huge strain on existing economic structures.

Dramatic shifts in business culture, where companies are forced to restructure themselves in response to tougher competition. This often involves the movement of employees to unfamiliar forms of employment, leading to reduced status or unemployment for those who are not able to adapt. The trend is towards 'virtual' organizations where all but core activities are contracted out. Although there are signs that employers are reconsidering the wisdom of this line of action, it seems highly unlikely that there will ever be a return to the stability of the past.

Despite the obvious trends, many people still consider a job-for-life the norm, and base all their plans on this expectation. What a blow, then, to find themselves faced with the increasingly common alternatives:

➡ temporary work
➡ long- or short-term contracts
➡ part-time jobs
➡ sclf-cmployment
➡ a mix of the above

Of course, flexible working patterns are by no means bad news for everyone. For instance, they allow mothers to plan work around home and family, although it sometimes means settling for low rates of pay and an erosion of career prospects.

At the other extreme, in the IT industry, where contract work is standard, 'techies' have the world at their fingertips. As long as professionals keep their skills up-to-date and can withstand the unremitting pressures of tight deadlines and unsocial hours, the financial rewards are enormous.

For the majority of people, however, the problem is the increasing erosion of *choice* in how they would like to organize their working life. Employers, too, are struggling to stay on top of challenging new work systems and the gaps left by downsizing (reducing the workforce), not least the need to motivate and retain their core of permanent staff whilst getting the best out of temporary and sub-contracted expertise.

Some of you may have already felt the impact of these trends. Consider the the following scenarios:

A You leap from your bed in the morning, full of energy and enthusiasm for the day ahead. Your electronic diary tells you that today your management consultancy skills are needed at an international bank. Later in the week, from the comfort of your own home, you will be running an on-line motivational course for executives in Europe, the US and Australia. Before donning your designer suit, you check the mail, which is bursting with letters from top companies anxious to secure your services at any price.

Ⓑ You crawl out of bed, dreading another day of drudgery at work, (it can be anywhere). Employed on a part-time contract for the lowest rates in the industry, you are surrounded by colleagues who are as depressed and demotivated as you. Always one step away from destitution, you are desperately trying to find a second job to top up your income. You don't bother to open the mail because you know it will be full of rejection letters from companies who consider your skills obsolete and your experience irrelevant to their needs.

In A we find the high-flying, self-employed consultant, established in a portfolio career, earning fat fees from a range of marketable skills and operating in the international arena, courtesy of the Internet. By contrast, B is the low-skilled, temporary worker forced to combine a number of low-paid part-time jobs merely to survive.

Does either of the above resemble your current situation? Perhaps you are somewhere in between, or perhaps you haven't even started out yet? It doesn't really matter. The point is that as we enter the millennium, the gap between winners and losers in the labour market is growing wider.

Whatever the individual's status or pay, the reality of work today is that many people are living with insecurity and being worked into the ground to meet impossible targets. In such a fast-changing environment, today's winners easily become tomorrow's losers.

Uncertainty about the the future affects people at all levels and in all industries. However, it is worth looking at our portfolio worker a little more closely to see what makes the essential difference between success and failure.

It is not just a matter of skills and qualifications. No, what this person has in abundance is the ability to anticipate *change* and seize opportunities. He or she is a powerhouse of energy, with an attitude of 'can do' in relation to new ideas and working methods. For whatever reason, this is what B lacks. Change in itself is neither good nor bad. Being neutral, it assumes the qualities we attribute to it. Hence, what one person finds exciting, another experiences as threatening.

Individuals and their reactions are all very different, but when problems arise, the common denominator is nearly always fear. Even the apparent winners suffer from anxiety about the future, and no matter what we achieve, it seems as though we are all in fear of losing it. Not even the people who get to the top are spared. They still have to constantly look over their shoulders, and watch their backs. Scratch the gilt-edged surface and you find the same old apprehensions. However successful we are, there is always the fear of losing everything. And what are the prizes that we work so desperately hard for?

In the traditional model of career success, we attain a position of importance in an organization and earn lots of money. So far, so good.

But what happens when the music stops? What sustains us when we have no time to spend with our families, grow older, fall sick or become victims of redundancy? In my experience, it is easier to address the financial problems than to help clients with the deeper questions, such as retaining a sense of worth when their job is snatched away or balancing long hours with an active life outside work.

Not long ago the Asian tiger economies were being hailed as the way forward for business in the millennium. Then what happened? Financial collapse, followed by 1929-style suicides in Japan, Hong Kong and Thailand. In these and other Asian countries, a new class has emerged, 'the formerly rich', among them the executives who have been forced to trade in their top-of-the-range cars, gold watches and cellular phones just to stay alive. On a less dramatic level, mergers and takeovers in the West have resulted in restructuring at all levels, with even the most successful people finding they cannot depend on telephone number salaries any longer.

Recessions come and go, and jobs along with them. For a while the economy is strong, then comes another global wobble, resurrecting the now familiar predictions of doom and gloom. The world has shrunk to such an extent that we can no longer ignore the plight of other countries; what happens in the East, Russia or anywhere else has very real implications for all of us. The only way to ride the storm is to learn to live with instability and be ready to cope with the inevitable twists and turns in our working lives.

You Exist for Yourself

As outward security erodes, many people are already looking for a new measure of prosperity. They want a life which allows them to go beyond the mundane, where they can balance financial and material needs with the opportunity for personal growth. This why they are giving more attention to adopting a healthier lifestyle, pursuing inner calm, and nourishing their relationships.

Once again, we are talking about the value of knowledge, but this time in its deepest sense. If you understand the importance of self-knowledge, you will never be battered and cast adrift by the storms of outside events.

The first thing to recognize is that you have an identity which is not defined by the work you do. It is a basic, but profound truth; *you do not exist for your work, you exist for yourself.*

Paradoxically, this makes re-inventing yourself in a professional sense much easier. You don't have to give up your ambitions, but you do have to let go of the slavish attachment to what other people think. Once you are setting your own goals for your own fulfilment, the thought of so-called failure isn't a problem any more. Worrying about our status and the symbols of success is hard work. As soon as we drop this unnecessary baggage, the sense of freedom becomes exhilarating.

Nor does letting go of the compulsive need to please others mean that we become more selfish. On the contrary, being at peace with ourselves makes us far more useful to those around us. The problem is not the desire to help our fellows, but the *compulsion* to be thought well of.

> *Take a few minutes now to think about what you want in your*
> *life. If you can see that there is a need to think beyond the*
> *conventional model of success, you have just taken the first step*
> *towards becoming a Millennium Candidate.*

We are far from being powerless victims of events going on around us. On the contrary, when we adopt a new approach in how we see our jobs, we are able to take back control of our lives.

This approach starts with identifying and harnessing an inner knowledge which goes beyond the influence of change. It means being able to access and use a very special state of consciousness, where you can experience the calmness and balance within; a state of *vibrant stillness*. When you are able to do this systematically, you will operate from a different base level, and keep your nerve despite the never-ending threats from outside.

This state of vibrant stillness represents energy at its most subtle level. It is unique because it does *not change*, and over time, its power becomes sustainable. Although characterized by a complete sense of calm, its vibrancy comes from its infinite potential.

Those who do martial arts have been systematically cultivating such an awareness for centuries. They know that once they achieve this essential balance, their efforts will become harmonious and spontaneous, greatly enhancing their chances of winning. For the master players it is seen as an essential prelude to combat, a philosophy that has obvious significance for those of us competing in the careers arena. However, the benefits are not confined to an elite few; they can be harnessed and used by anyone.

Nor is there is anything strange or frightening about this form of awareness; we all experience it from time to time. Have you ever found yourself immersed in a pleasurable activity, to the point where you are completely unaware of time passing? If the answer is 'yes', then you have already experienced what I am describing. Listening to music is one of the most common examples for people who don't practise any specific awareness raising techniques.

Think about it now. Have you ever been engrossed in an enjoyable activity where you lost all sense of time, and came back feeling refreshed and strong? Make a note of these experiences below:

I experienced this when I:

....

....

....

....

....

This is the field where your creative impulses originate; it is the source of the hunches and intuition so important to career success. It's why you can burn the midnight oil trying to solve a complex problem, only to find the answer comes of its own accord as you lie in bed. But this process doesn't have to be left to chance; it can be consciously accelerated and used to your advantage, something we will explore in the next chapter.

What the sports example illustrates is that it is possible to have gain without pain. If you can accept this, you will be laying the foundation for all the other techniques in this book. The underlying principle is that success does not come from physical and mental *exertion* alone. Hard work will pay dividends, but you don't have to suffer in the process.

Inward Investment

To illustrate how inner harmony can work in your favour, let me share a personal experience with you. For eleven years, I worked at IBM, where I enjoyed a good salary, a variety of highly motivating perks and a stimulating working environment. However, over time, I realized that my real satisfaction came not from my 'day job', but from the voluntary work I did on behalf of the company. Finally, when the circumstances were right, I used this experience to set up as a self-employed careers consultant.

And then a strange thing happened. Although I was financially secure and had plenty of time at my disposal, a sense of isolation overtook me, and I began to entertain the idea of going back into another job very like the one I had just left. Why? Because peer pressure had set in, and for a while I made the common mistake of thinking I gave up my identity with my job.

Fortunately, I soon came to my senses and accepted that I had taken on a very different pattern of work, where I could no longer fall back on the borrowed status of belonging to a world-renowned corporation. I also realized that the systematic practice of deep relaxation techniques was the key to my survival as a lone operator. This *inward investment* proved to be the most important step on the road to a new fulfilling career.

One word of caution, however. Accessing this energy is not the same as experiencing the effects of recreational drugs. The debate on the damage they do versus the supposed benefits is not for discussion here. The important issue is that the drug-induced feelings are not sustainable; they last only while the user is under the influence of the drug.

Yet another way to access our deeper levels of understanding is to consult the ancient works of wisdom from the East, whose messages are every bit as relevant to today's readers as they were to the ancients. Like us, they lived in turbulent and revolutionary times, and were constantly seeking to make sense of what was happening in their lives.

When economic and technological changes come under discussion, you can be sure that the word 'revolution' will come into the debate sooner or later. Corporations and business gurus frequently describe the 'revolution' in the world of work, while governments argue the merits of a 'revolution' in international finance. Although this may convey energy and excitement to some, it can also breed instability and fear.

However, there is an alternative definition of the word which puts the whole business of transformation, even upheaval, into a more balanced perspective. In this other sense, 'revolution' means nothing more than 'going round'.

We think of the eruptions in the outer world as new, but this is not the case. Our contemporary problems are essentially the same as they have been through the ages. Life has always been a struggle in one form or another; it's only the outward forms that differ.

In business and politics, as elsewhere, fashions come and go. Predictions for the future abound, along with a host of guidance systems to help us survive in challenging times. Many of these soon wither on the vine, but others survive because they offer a timeless truth.

One of the most cherished of these enduring systems is the Tao Te Ching, a work which has been used for thousands of years by scholars and lay people alike. In providing a liberating interpretation of revolution, it can only become more influential with future generations. According to legend it was written by Lao Tze in 6th-century China. Both profound and down to earth, it has been a source of inspiration and practical help for those seeking personal growth or business success. It continues to be the subject of much study by philosophers and psychologists, and has become an enduring element of professional development training.

The Tao does not offer advice, but a path by which individuals can get in touch with their intuitive side. There are a number of translations and commentaries, but it is left to readers to interpret how it can meet their individual needs.

Ultimately the Tao is about *self-awareness*; how we can harness inner powers and influence our surroundings by tuning into the evolutionary forces of nature. This allows us to take decisions and bring about changes more harmoniously. Once we are in step with universal energy, known in traditional terms as the 'life force', we can achieve our desires with a minimum of physical and mental effort, and begin to enjoy the full support of nature in our work.

In the pages of the Tao Te Ching you will find a perfect illustration of the 'gain without pain' approach to life. In encouraging acceptance of personal cause and effect, it presents a liberating alternative to the 'blame them' philosophy, an outlook that will be fatal in the next century. According to the Tao's model, 'It's not them, it's ME!' Instead of criticizing others and outward circumstances, we examine our own shortcomings first, then look at how we can influence external factors.

Taking responsibility for our actions in this way does not devalue the benefits of modern self-improvement tools, nor does it entail becoming passive or accepting abuse from others. Rather, it means breaking free from destructive thinking and clearing away the debris of conditioned responses. If you accept this, then you will see that the real revolution in the world of work will be driven by individuals who have learned to balance the profusion of external information with the liberating wealth of knowledge within.

Many people find this a challenging concept, because in the West our thinking tends to be dominated by logic. According to neurologists, this type of thinking draws on the functions of the left hemisphere of the brain. The Tao Te Ching and other traditional Chinese texts do not contradict the logical approach, but add a further dimension by also encouraging us to release our intuition, a function of the right hemisphere of the brain. In this way, we can enjoy the benefits of both sides working in harmony.

For instance, have you ever noticed that there are times in your life when everything goes right for you? This is usually attributed to luck, but I have witnessed people creating their own 'luck' every day. Hard work certainly helps, but how do we explain the hunch factor? I have seen measurable improvements in results when individuals are able to balance their mental and physical exertions with some form of structured relaxation technique.

If these ideas are new to you, it may be worth setting aside some specific time to give them more thought before moving on.

Keep in mind that this is not about indulging flights of fancy or wishful thinking, but a matter of down-to-earth commonsense. Think about it – throughout your career you will face a variety of appointments, interviews, business meetings, networking opportunities and social gatherings. All I am asking you to do at this stage is to take some time out before plunging into any more engagements. Why not make an appointment with *yourself* for a change?

In the future, as in the past, the ultimate winners will be those who discover their true identity, one that cannot be undermined by external dramas. We may ride high for a while on the back of outward strengths, but the sum of our achievements counts for nothing if we cannot cope with the inevitability of material loss.

In the next chapter I will share some of the deep relaxation techniques my clients and associates have used, but right now I would like you to try a very simple exercise as a primer.

Even now as you are reading, you may be experiencing muscular tension. Stop for a while and do a quick body check. Sit still and become aware of your posture. For instance, how are you holding this book? Are your fingers clenched? Shoulders hunched? Is your jaw tight? Breathe in gently, and on the outward breath, be aware of all the tension leaving your body.

Whatever your current situation or aspirations, what we have covered so far will provide a platform for everything else you do. In this book you will find an abundance of guidance to help you on your way, but no amount of learned techniques can replace the natural strength that comes from being comfortable with yourself. Bosses, interviewers, colleagues and all the others you want to influence will sense the power that comes from regularly dipping into your inner knowledge. This is the starting point of making yourself valuable.

SUMMARY

* The world of work is changing dramatically, creating a culture of winners and losers.
* The winners will be those who make themselves valuable to the decision makers.
* Making time to nourish inner growth is central to the millennium model of success.
* To create your own luck you must regularly experience the creative energy within.
* Learning to value our true self is the key to convincing others of our worth.

Chapter Two

From Stress to Success

The stressful events in our life are
not the problem. The problem is
how we respond to them.

Your Levels of Stress

The company has just reorganized and word is out that you are in
line for the axe. Your heart beats faster, your blood pressure rises
and your muscles become tense. Sound familiar? You are experiencing stress.

Stress is the greatest barrier to accessing the creative awareness
so vital to success in the millennium. It also starves us of energy
and is the chief culprit when we lose our nerve in challenging situations. Given the high levels of insecurity in today's job market, it
should come as no surprise that stress management needs to be a
major part of your Campaign Plan. This applies whether you are
in or out of work.

The first step is to understand exactly what we mean by
'stress'. The word is commonly used to mean anxiety or tension,
but it can also be applied to:

The unpleasant *physiological symptoms* above, arising from
the fight or flight response that often overtakes us when we are
threatened by events which are out of our control. Adrenaline
and other chemicals are being released into our body, but
because we are unlikely to bare our fists or take physical flight,
we can stay wound up for much longer than is good for us.

Stress can be caused by:

Events (also known as 'stressors') that range from bereavement to job-hunting.

But even this is only to look at the the negative aspects. To get the full picture, we also need to consider the indispensable role of positive stress in our lives. 'Good' stress is absolutely essential, not just for our survival, but as the driver of our creativity, excitement and passion. How could we compete in sports or square up to a confrontational exchange without the stimulus of stress? In these circumstances, it's perfectly natural to feel a degree of tension, with an accompanying rush of adrenaline. In fact, these are the very things that carry us through.

So what makes the difference between the negative and the positive? The difficulties only arise when we overshoot our personal tolerance level, and it is this negative aspect of stress that we are concerned with in this chapter.

To demonstrate the importance of the personal perspective, I always start my workshops by dividing participants into two teams, asking one group to produce a list of situations that trigger bad stress and the other to record the experiences that stimulate and motivate them. Here are some of the contrasting results:

- 'Losing my job crushed my self-esteem.'
- 'Being made redundant was the best thing that ever happened to me.'

- 'Job search is tiring and demoralizing.'
- 'Having to go out and look for work has brought me out of my shell.'

- 'Deadlines get me into a panic.'
- 'I perform better when I'm under pressure.'

- 'Too much work is making me ill.'
- 'Sometimes I take on too much, but it gives me a buzz.'

- 'Not having other people around is my main problem at work.'
- 'I find it much easier to work on my own.'

Clearly, the same situation can motivate one person whilst provoking anxiety in another. This shows us that the events in our life are not the problem. The problem is how we respond to them. For instance, some people like a lot of stimulation, others prefer the quiet life.

Obviously it is not only in the workplace that we encounter pressure. We are all programmed to worry, and on losing our job, we simply exchange one set of insecurities for another. For example, fears about meeting targets and being a wage-slave are replaced by worry over shortage of money and relegation to the ranks of the unemployed. Young people often lose sleep over their exams and job prospects, while older people fret about how they will cope with retirement.

The internal dialogue never stops, and carried along by the habitual impulse to keep going at any price, we become trapped in a vicious circle. Taking action while under stress creates further stress, and so on, as illustrated below:

The Vicious Circle

Stress

Action

Result: pressure builds up

This is how stress takes hold, and over time it becomes harder and harder to break the vicious circle.

This cycle affects us mentally and physically. Prolonged exposure to stress impairs our capabilities, makes us tired and threatens our confidence. Many physical disorders and diseases are thought to be associated with the body's reaction to stress, including tension headaches, allergies and strokes.

In recent years it has become one of the biggest industrial diseases, costing employers billions in lost time, legal settlements and drops in efficiency. The problem is not going to go away, and it will continue to be a major issue in the millennium.

Some people are so caught up in the vicious circle that they are totally unaware of being under pressure. Those around them are quicker to spot the giveaway signs; the bad-tempered outbursts, the nail-biting, finger-drumming, and a host of other irritating habits. Obviously employers notice these compulsions as well, so if you are serious about becoming a Millennium Candidate, it's vital to put your own behaviour to the test.

Are you showing signs of stress? Take some time now to check yourself out, using the questionnaire below as a guide. Don't cheat. Only by being scrupulously honest will you find out what you need to work on.

Do you suffer from any of the following:

Mental symptoms of stress

- [ ] constant irritability with people
- [ ] feeling unable to cope
- [ ] a sense of being a failure
- [ ] difficulty in making decisions
- [ ] awareness of suppressed anger
- [ ] difficulty in letting go or laughing
- [ ] problems with relaxing
- [ ] dread of the future
- [ ] resistance to feedback
- [ ] inability to finish one task before starting another

Physical signs of stress

- [ ] heart palpitations
- [ ] fainting, dizziness or sweating
- [ ] indigestion, stomach ache
- [ ] nervous twitching and trembling
- [ ] headaches or migraine
- [ ] persistent tiredness
- [ ] insomnia
- [ ] lack of appetite

Habits

Do you:

- [ ] drink too much alochol?
- [ ] smoke heavily?
- [ ] drink coffee to excess?
- [ ] take tranquillizers?
- [ ] eat for comfort?
- [ ] bite your nails?

Any one, or combination, of the above, could be an indication of undue pressure building up. The list is not exhaustive, so add your own observations. These may also be a warning of physical or mental illness, so don't hesitate to get medical help if you have any doubts.

Now let's look at what might be causing anxiety in your life, starting with what's happening on the outside. Do any of the following 'stressors' apply to you?

- [ ] job-hunting
- [ ] loss of status due to job loss
- [ ] lack of funds and resources
- [ ] fragmented work patterns

- [ ] lack of skills
- [ ] overwork
- [ ] family problems
- [ ] bereavement
- [ ] an accumulation of minor irritations

> Make a note below of anything causing you excessive worry at the moment:
>
> ....
> ....
> ....
> ....
> ....
> ....

The simple process of listing problems may well help you to see the way forward to putting them right. Of course, there will be other things that are not so easily dealt with, which is why you will find a suggested action plan at the end of the chapter.

Then there is the matter of attitude. There have been a variety of studies by psychologists over the years, but it will come as no surprise to find that persistently resentful individuals are the front-runners in the anxiety stakes. Those who would rather blame others than put their own negative behaviour to the test not only allow tensions to accumulate, but often find themselves isolated. People simply don't want to be around whingers. Without anyone to confide in, the 'blamer' becomes introspective and prone to depression, with predictable results.

There is no suggestion that you are like this, but can you in all honesty say that your attitude and behaviour would not benefit from a little work? In the short term, we can't always influence the people and events in our lives, but there is always scope to work on ourselves. Think about it now. Can you accept that we ultimately create our own reality?

Addressing this question becomes even more urgent when we

lose a job. Of course, it's easy to blame the organization, the government or even society. While any one or all of these may be responsible, the real issue is what are *you* going to do about it? In the long term, you may be able to influence the external forces, but in the short term the least painful solution is to take responsibility for yourself and get down to action.

You may also encounter individuals who argue that occupational stress is merely a myth, a term used as an excuse for poor leadership and inefficient work systems. Certainly, the word can be misused, but there is no disguising the reality of the negative inner reaction to these outward circumstances. Whatever we choose to call it, the growth of fear and worry in the workplace is real, and left to itself, is not going to go away.

Obviously if someone is working under impossible conditions, this must be the first problem to be tackled. The exhausted retail manager working eighty hours a week did not want to hear that he should set aside more time for inner contemplation. No, the immediate priority was a new job, and that's what he got.

Another view is that stress management is for wimps, but those who make such claims rarely bother to get to the heart of the matter. This is a mistake, because having a successful career is largely about establishing good relationships, and for that you need to have a good relationship with *yourself*. That means having the courage to put your motivation and behaviour under closer scrutiny, something the detractors would never have the courage to do.

Of course, there are individuals of a naturally cheerful and balanced disposition, who are less susceptible to anxiety than the rest of us. However, if you are one of these fortunate people, you will still need to give your mental faculties a regular break if you want to allow your spontaneous creativity to surface.

Having established what stress means and how it affects us personally, we can turn our attention to handling it. In the previous chapter, we saw that learning from the past can help us plan the future, but it is equally true that when it comes to action, all we have at our disposal is 'now'. At this very moment, you have the power to stop and reflect, then plan how you are going to unwind on a regular basis.

Start by doing the body scan in Chapter One again, and get used to doing it at intervals throughout the day. It takes less than a minute, and it's unlikely that anyone will notice. Make the most of enforced breaks, like sitting at traffic lights or waiting in a queue.

Now spend some more time thinking about the routine activities that may be causing you to tense your muscles. These may include:

➤ driving
➤ typing
➤ sitting in a meeting
➤ writing
➤ using the phone

Make your list here:

....

....

....

....

....

....

You will be amazed at what hard work we make of simple tasks, but after a while you should be able to anticipate what triggers the tension, and find it easier to loosen up.

If you make these body scans part of your regular routine, it won't take long to put things right, and there is no shortage of helpful books and audio tapes on the subject. However, if you suspect more serious problems, you may need the help of a physiotherapist or other specialist.

If poor posture is your problem, you might want to try the Alexander Technique. I have had many excellent reports on its effectiveness. Frederick Alexander was an actor, and his system of developing coordination throughout the body, and 'unlearning' bad habits is still used by actors around the world. It is equally popular with individuals outside the profession, particularly those with back pain. I'm told that improvement starts straight away, and you should also feel healthier and more confident. You can book one-to-one coaching or join a class.

From now on, whenever you feel the tension mounting try an instant calmer. Here's one that's a variation on the exercise in Chapter One:

> Stop. Breathe in deeply. Breathe out slowly, allowing your shoulders to drop gently. Breathe in again, checking your body for tension. Breathe out slowly, relaxing your tense muscles at the same time. Take a few more gentle breaths.

This very basic exercise can work wonders, and takes less than 30 seconds. Just one word of caution. When I say 'breathe deeply', I don't mean take rasping breaths, but simply inhale a little more deeply than usual.

Now make a note of the ways you normally relax:

You have probably included some of the following:

- watching television
- sport
- reading
- taking holidays
- physical exercise
- socializing

All of the above are natural and useful ways to combat surface stress, but only structured relaxation techniques will allow you to activate more profound energy levels and achieve sustainable results. The only effective way to stop the build-up of pressure and accelerate your intuitive powers is to make deep relaxation a part of your daily routine. Over time, this will break the vicious circle, and you will find a new energizing cycle taking its place:

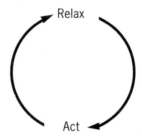

Relax

Act

Result: sustainable energy,
heightened creativity

By regularly dipping into our deeper consciousness, we are able to refresh our thought processes and systematically reduce our anxiety levels. Our future actions are then built on an increasingly strong foundation, with the result that the adverse impact of external conditions decreases. We are less inclined to internalize problems and our work gradually becomes easier and more productive. Put simply, we get better results and conserve more energy. This is how you will be able to experience the reality of *doing less to achieve more.*

Of course, whatever techniques are used, stress does not disappear altogether, nor would we want it to. However, with regular practice, mobilising the good stress becomes easier, and the bad starts to lose its grip.

Guide to Techniques and Therapies

The best way to achieve deep relaxation is to use a mind–body technique, which works on the principle that the mind affects the body and vice versa. Some of these are drawn from time-tested Eastern philosopies, and others are modern in origin. Below is a brief summary of some of the methods which have proved successful for me, my clients and my business associates. You may find them helpful in making a choice for yourself.

Transcendental Meditation (TM)

I started to use TM, as taught by Maharishi Mahesh Yogi, many years ago because I was impressed by the number of business people who achieved measurable results with it. I also liked the sound scientific research it offers to back its claim that those who practise it reach an expanded state of mental and spiritual awareness. From my own experience, I can confirm that meditators are able to go beyond thought, and reach a quiet place where the constant hub of inner chatter subsides. The benefits of accessing this state of vibrant stillness have proved themselves to me time and again in work and personal situations. It is uncomplicated and does not involve concentration, trances or subscribing to any particular belief system, unless the practitioner wants to explore its origins further. For me, its greatest attraction is its simplicity.

That TM works so well for me does not mean it will have the same appeal to you, so now let's examine some of the other methods people use.

Breath Control

There is a direct link between breathing and relaxation. Using calm, controlled breathing in a threatening situation – for example before an interview – can be very soothing. Although it is most effective when used as part of other meditation or yogic techniques, people have also found it helpful on its own. This is not surprising, as breath control has been practised for thousand of years, and is one of the most powerful transformational tools available.

Yoga

Yoga is one of the most popular methods I have come across. For some, it becomes a way of life; others view it as a gentle form of keep-fit. Although best known for teaching the correct way to breathe and perform a variety of calming physical movements, it can also include meditation. It originated in India, and is known to be at least 4,000 years old. The word yoga means 'union', in the sense of being at ease with one's self and one's surroundings. It is not about standing on your head for hours or sitting on the floor with your legs tied in knots. It can be practised from a chair, or in bed if necessary, and is often used as part of a pain control regime by people suffering from chronic ill-health.

Audio tapes

These are easy to use and can be very effective. They may involve an activity, such as alternately tensing and relaxing the muscles, or simply allow you to listen to soothing music or sounds from nature. Others may use guided visualizations or various types of chanting. You can even learn Clinically Standardized Meditation (CSM) with the help of an audio tape and a step-by-step instruction manual.

T'ai-chi Ch'uan

This system springs from the Taoist principles of harmonizing activities with natural events, which was explained in Chapter One. Being physical in nature, it has obvious appeal to those who prefer relaxing through movement, rather than by sitting still. It is practised slowly and smoothly, with the carefully aligned postures accompanied by coordinated breathing.

Aromatherapy

Aromatherapy sets out to promote a sense of well-being through the inhalation and massage of essential oils, derived from plants chosen for their therapeutic qualities. These can be stimulating, refreshing or sedative. The oils are absorbed into the skin as a qualified therapist massages the body. You can also add oils to bathwater, inhale them or use them for skin preparations. Applied in the wrong proportions they can be toxic, so be warned if you are thinking of mixing your own. For beginners, it is best to stick to ready-made preparations.

These are just a few of many routes to inner harmony, and where meditation and massage are concerned, there are a variety of types to choose from, so you are certainly not limited to the above.

The best way to check whether something will work for you is to try it. A good teacher or therapist should also be prepared to answer your questions before anything definite is booked. Qualifications are important, so make sure you ask about these. A properly qualified professional will also adhere to the code of ethics of any regulating body, an important protection for you.

Some people find that their religion is the key factor in overcoming stress, and they find it hard to see why anything else is needed. My response to this is that deep relaxation techniques tend to enhance religious experience rather than interfering with it.

Even people of no particular faith are moving ever closer to incorporating a spiritual dimension into their lives. This accounts for the popularity of religious retreat centres, where people can take time out to achieve a degree of tranquillity before plunging back into their frantic work routines.

At other times, people need that bit of extra help to get them through major life changes, such as bereavement or losing a job. In these cases, seeing a qualified counsellor can be helpful. However, the ultimate aim of counselling is to empower you to handle difficult situations on your own, and you should never use it as a prop that allows you stay in the role of victim.

If you have a disability or a physical or mental health condition, your doctor may have an opinion about the benefits or drawbacks of any particular method. For instance, meditation may not be a good choice for anyone with a history of mental illness. Conversely, if you have a physical disability, it may be the ideal solution.

There is usually a cost involved in learning a particular system or going to a complementary therapist. Whether you can afford it is really a matter of priorities. If you want to reap the rewards, you will have to weigh the costs against other expenses. I hope by now it won't be difficult to choose between this and any other leisure or luxury items on your list of needs. What better investment could you make for the future?

For those of you who like subjective experiences to be backed up by objective studies, the scientific evidence for the effectiveness of mind-body techniques is growing, as researchers continue with controlled experiments to support what people report.

One of the most encouraging findings is that people who practise meditation regularly have high levels of alpha brainwave activity. This is significant because alpha waves are linked to pleasure and creativity, and they are only active when the subject is both relaxed and receptive to what is going on around them. This rules out any question of going into a trance, which is why I describe the deeply relaxed state as a vibrant stillness. Interestingly, sports people have also been found to have this same alpha wave activity at crucial moments of concentration.

Perhaps the biggest step forward is a growing receptivity to complementary approaches in the mainstream medical profession. Some doctors even have therapists working alongside them.

Unless you have some pressing problems to resolve first, I suggest that from now on you set aside some time to practise a deep relaxation technique in a systematic way each day. This will be in addition to the things you normally do, like watching television. The short awareness and breathing exercises are a good way to start, but they in themselves won't be enough to activate profound creative energy levels.

Your plan should include talking to anyone else in your life who may be affected by your new routine.

Think now about when and where you could find some peace and quiet, then schedule some specific times to get started. Always make sure the room is well ventilated and that your clothes are loose and comfortable.

Date/Time	Who else is affected?	What do I need to organize?

Changing the habits of a lifetime will take dedication and discipline. Establish a programme in the same way that you would prepare for a project at work or revise for an exam.

There is no need to go overboard and sit in comtemplation all day. The objective is to achieve a balance between action and rest. For meditation, 20 minutes morning and evening is ideal, although 30 minutes once a day would still produce good results. For this or any other system, you should ultimately be guided by your instructor or therapist. You can do more if you want to get away for a while to a special centre, where guidance and support are available. When using audio tapes, stick to the guidelines in the instructions for use.

Always take time to resurface before resuming everyday activities, or you could give your system a nasty shock. To ease yourself back, try something physical, like stretching and yawning.

The 3 Rs of Success

The secret of your new stress management routine lies in being faithful to the 3 Rs:

Relax
Refresh
Resume

This way your problems won't have the opportunity to accumulate and do you harm.

At this stage, instead of trying to consciously suppress negative feelings and habits, which will only compound your problems in the short term, use the 3 Rs to establish a natural healthy pattern of behaviour. Soon you will find that many of your problems will begin to take care of themselves.

Later on, when you are adept at accessing and incorporating sustainable energy into your daily activities, you will be ready to experiment with some of the positive thinking exercises outlined in this book. These can be very enjoyable, but are only effective if you don't strain to get successful outcomes.

However, before we go any further, you also need to be aware of a phenomenon known to complementary therapists as the 'healing crisis'. This is a period when practising deep relaxation can make you feel worse before feeling better. For instance, in the early days, you may feel tired, experience a few physical aches and pains, or come out in a rash. Emotional responses might produce a sense of gloom or tearfulness. This is because as the body starts to de-stress it also begins to rid itself of toxins and the mind effectively does the same.

These experiences are quite normal and should pass, although having professional help to hand will provide you with a safety net. (This is the main disadvantage of using audio tapes in isolation.) It's unlikely that symptoms will be extreme, unless there are some deep-rooted problems coming to the surface. As ever, if you are really worried, seek medical guidance.

After a few weeks of practice, you will start to feel an increased mental alertness and find that your stamina is improving. As time goes on, you will see exactly what I mean by *gain without pain* and *creating your own luck*. Of course you will still have problems, but your attitude towards them will change.

Eventually you will find that you do indeed have an identity which cannot be shaken by the events around you. Even the most fleeting glimpse of your own inner harmony can take away so much fear and needless worry.

With regard to your outer circumstances, the golden rule is to get organized. Once you take control of your own development and know how to keep abreast of world trends, you are already a long way down the road to coping with instability.

Personal Action Plan Options

- [ ] Examine the things that are putting you under pressure, and decide what can be tackled now, and what may take longer.
- [ ] Get help from others if you need it, for example, family, doctor, therapist, careers adviser.
- [ ] Identify a mind-body technique that suits you and schedule regular slots to practise – see Appendix One for book list.
- [ ] Learn how to manage your time effectively – see Chapter Four.
- [ ] Don't be afraid to delegate.
- [ ] Work on being more assertive – see Chapter Five.
- [ ] Take regular physical exercise if you have the capability – see Chapter Three.

☐ Plan a healthy diet – see Chapter Three.

☐ If you're unhappy at work, look at options like retraining or changing jobs – see Chapters Seven to Twelve.

☐ Work on making your surroundings comfortable.

☐ Learn and practise positive thinking – see Chapter Six.

☐ Nourish your personal and professional relationships – see Chapter Five.

☐ Plan at least one and a half days each week away from normal work routines.

☐ Don't miss out on an annual holiday (even if you're not able to go away).

☐ Join a stress management class, where you can share problems and ideas with others.

Add your own ideas:

....

....

....

....

....

....

Although certain chapters have been outlined as relevant to particular options, the whole of this book could be described as a stress management guide.

SUMMARY

* Stress management is a key factor in coping with the insecurity of today's job market.
* With regular practice, we can learn to identify our personal stress 'triggers', and take preventative action.
* Systematic use of deep-relaxation techniques is the key to managing

pressure and building up a healthy pattern of behaviour.

* You can chose from a wide range of techniques, from meditation to aromatherapy.

Chapter Three

Fit for the Millennium

In the millennium, fitness and
health issues will be central to the
workplace culture.

Health versus Fitness

Having learned how to mobilize your inner energy, the next step
is to focus on shaping up physically with a customized health and
fitness plan.

Keeping fit has been fashionable for a long time, and we all
know we must limber up to look good and ward off disease. But
when it comes to climbing the career ladder and enlivening your
job search, there are some very specific reasons to make good
health a priority. Consider the following:

➧ your physical and mental performance will improve.
➧ your stress management programme will be enhanced.
➧ your activities will look good on your CV (résumé).
➧ you will make a strong first impression in interviews.

All of this adds up to a significant competitive edge in the workplace. Without doubt, looking after yourself boosts your value to
employers. Like it or not, fitness has become a key factor in pro-
jecting a professional image. No wonder high-flyers are increasingly finding time for structured exercise and sport!

The reasons are even more compelling if you turn your attention to the future world of work. Demands on your nerve and
stamina will accelerate as you learn to stay on top of:

➧ fragmented and mobile working patterns

- national and international travel
- widening networks of business relationships
- multi-tasking and continual retraining

You won't have to be a world-class athlete, but you will have to be ready to cope with change and movement as a matter of course. Unless you prepare yourself now, all this could take a heavy toll on you physically as well as increasing your stress levels.

Many people talk of health and fitness as if they are the same, but this is not the case. Sweating it out at the gym twice a week may make you physically fit, but are you healthy? Let's look at the difference.

Health. Good health includes fitness, but is much wider in scope. It requires an understanding of what causes illness and the part lifestyle plays in the process.

Fitness. All round physical fitness includes:

- flexibility
- strength
- stamina

You need muscular *flexibility* and *strength* to keep you mobile and allow you to bend and stretch without injuring yourself. *Stamina* keeps your lungs and heart healthy, and helps you to summon extra energy, for instance when you need to run for the train or climb several flights of stairs.

Interestingly, some health specialists think it can be the little things that count when it comes to fitness. They say it is quite possible for the mother, with no time for a work-out, to keep in shape by looking after home and children. This regular activity could even make her fitter than a dedicated gym user.

Testing Your Health and Fitness

You will know that you are out of shape if you find yourself getting out of breath and tired while performing everyday activities. However, to get a comprehensive assessment, you will need to consult a specialist from time to time.

Healthclubs and gyms can give you a fitness test, but the best way to keep track of your overall health is to have a full medical check-up with a health care company. You can expect to be put through a wide variety of medical tests, including a complete physical examination by a doctor. Other checks should include:

- Exercises to assess your flexibility, stamina and strength.
- Pulse rate – to check how effectively the heart is pumping blood around the body.
- Cholesterol levels – to test whether you are at risk of heart disease for genetic or dietary reasons.
- Lung function – to check efficiency and detect any chest problems, like asthma.
- Blood pressure – to check stress levels and risk of a heart attack.
- Vision and hearing tests.
- Assessment of weight in relation to height.

You may also be assigned a personal adviser, who will help you to assess any lifestyle changes that will put you on the road to better health.

If you doubt the need for tests, here's some food for thought. A British Airways survey into the life-expectancy of 7,000 male pilots, carried out from 1950 to 1992, revealed them to be among the healthiest employees in Britain, suggesting that people with strict medical requirements for their job live up to five years longer than the general population. Regular assessments are also understood to have saved the lives of many by revealing that they were suffering from potentially fatal complaints.

A sad contrast to this is the case of the redundant factory worker who died of a suspected heart attack at the age of sixty-three, only two years after winning millions in a national lottery. Although he upgraded his house and car, he neglected to do the same for his health. Already suffering from heart trouble at the time of his win, he carried on with a sedentary lifestyle, regularly downing pints of beer, smoking and eating junk food.

Once again, we are looking at priorities. Medical check-ups may seem costly in the short term, but what price do you put on your longevity?

Lifestyle Assessment

If a head-to-toe assessment is really beyond your means at the moment, put the idea into your bring-forward file and settle for some less costly precautions in the meantime. Start by making your own analysis of your current lifestyle, using the following questionnaire as a guide.

Do you:

- take regular physical exercise?
- avoid smoking and drinking or keep it to a minimum?
- understand the basic rules of healthy eating?
- get sufficient sleep and wake up feeling refreshed?
- make time to unwind and practise deep relaxation?
- get plenty of exposure to fresh air and daylight?

How do you shape up? If you can see any room for improvement, read on.

Your Personal Health Plan

Before embarking on any health and fitness programme, test it first against the ABC guide. Is it:

Appropriate?
Balanced?
Consistent?

What's appropriate for a young person may be too demanding for someone in middle life, and the amount of exercise suitable for a worker in a sedentary job will probably be greater than that for a person doing more physically strenuous work. If you have a background of medical problems, your doctor will also have an opinion on what will help or hinder you.

Making sure your regime is balanced is equally important. Playing squash once a week and regularly pounding the treadmill are unlikely to keep you healthy if you ignore your diet and don't get enough rest.

And finally, consistency. So many worthy ideas find their way on to the scrap heap after a few short bursts of frenetic activity. Be honest, how many times have you made a New Year's resolution to get into shape, only to drop it long before Easter arrives?

With the ABC guide firmly in mind, let's look at the elements of a healthy lifestyle more closely.

Exercise

You can choose from a wide range of activities, depending on your starting point, personal preferences and budget. Apart from any recommendations or reservations your doctor may have, only *you* know what will be suitable.

Health Clubs

Let's start with the option of going to a gym or health club. This is not just about keeping in good condition and warding off disease, but about cultivating a strong and healthy appearance, something that has obvious appeal to employers.

It also has proven psychological advantages. Many people, from all walks of life, have told me that the discipline of going somewhere on a regular basis keeps them motivated and boosts their self-esteem, not least when they are between jobs. They also take advantage of the opportunities to socialize and network, which adds even further to the 'feelgood' factor.

When I complimented one of my business associates on his

ability to manage a huge workload with such good humour and balance, he attributed a good part of his success to twice-weekly visits to the gym. Even something as mundane as 20 minutes on a rowing machine has a direct bearing on his performance at work. The rhythmic exercise frees up his mind, allowing some of his most creative ideas to surface, and he has become far more disciplined in applying himself to the more routine aspects of his job.

Clubs offer a range of facilities, equipment and programmes, from rowing machines to multi-gyms, and of course aerobics classes. Again, it will require a financial investment, so it's worth doing an exploratory trip before signing up. Check out that the establishment has:

➠ Good parking facilities or public transport links.
➠ Well-qualified instructors, who are on top of the latest developments and can advise on a programme to match your ability.
➠ Well-maintained, up-to-date equipment, with a range of machines to vary your activities.
➠ An atmosphere where you will feel safe and comfortable.

You may also want to look for additional facilities, like a swimming pool, tennis court, saunas, and the services of qualified masseurs and beauticians.

If you are thinking about moving home, why not check out an apartment building with on-site facilities? You may find that running costs are included in the service charges and work out cheaper than going to an outside gym.

Personal Trainers

Some people hate the idea of exercising in public, but lack the motivation to work out at home. If you can afford it, one solution is to buy your own equipment and book a personal trainer who will be discreet about your pink, perspiring body. They are also highly skilled in keeping you motivated, and unlikely to let you off the hook because you 'don't feel like it'.

If the thought of bringing a stranger into your home fills you with horror, you could try an Internet service. For anyone linked to the Internet, a personal trainer need only be a mouse click away. For a monthly or annual fee, a certified professional will evaluate your health status then suggest programmes to suit your lifestyle, including weight loss and stress management.

Other Options

If you want something that's kinder on your budget, here are some activities that you can do on your own or with friends:

Walking is a good way to start if you are not used to regular exercise. It is safe and allows you to be flexible. You could begin by walking to work, building up over time to a brisk walk for half an hour or so. Make sure you wear comfortable shoes.

Swimming exercises all the muscle groups, and is recommended for most people, irrespective of age or physical ability.

Jogging is an excellent aerobic exercise, but it can put strain on your joints, so may be one to avoid if you are overweight or have arthritis. If you do go ahead, invest in running shoes with shock absorbers.

Cycling will keep you fit, but to optimize the benefits you should try to go at a good speed for at least 20 minutes at a time.

Team sports appeal to many people because they provide the added incentive of competition and the opportunity to spend time with friends. They also impress employers because team activity is seen as a positive indicator of how you will perform in a job.

Golf lessons might prove a sound investment on your way to the top. It's not only excellent exercise, but an ideal way to network with company executives.

Obviously, you can choose any sport that appeals to you, but check first that it will not be doing you any damage.

Yoga and *T'ai Chi* offer a gentle approach to physical fitness, as well as allowing the mind to become attuned to finer energies.

Whatever exercise you choose, the golden rule is to start slowly and build up. You can begin at any age, but if you are out of shape, over forty, or have any medical problems, check with your doctor before changing your routine. Other important points are: never push to exhaustion, warm up first, and take time to wind down. Remember, too, that pain is your body's way of saying stop, so ignore it at your peril. Your career plans will take a battering if you sustain joint or back injuries which may haunt you for the rest of your life.

How do you measure up when it comes to exercise? How much have you managed over the last 7 days? Make a note below. Don't forget to include everyday activities, like walking to work or playing with the children, but only if you can honestly say they are helping you to keep fit.

....

....

....

....

....

....

If you think you could be doing more, use the table at the end of this chapter to get started on an action plan.

If you have limited capability for physical exercise because of disability or a medical condition, this should not prevent you from impressing companies with your *fitness to do the job*. As we have seen, society puts a high price on physical image, and some disabled people face particular barriers to employment. This is a fact which cannot be ignored, and I have covered it in more detail in Part Two, dealing with job search.

In the meantime, if you are in this situation and facing an interview, approach any reservations from an employer from a position of inner strength by making sure you stay calm and collected. Challenge disabling attitudes by emphasizing your abilities, rather than allowing an interviewer to dwell on any perceived limitations.

It would, of course, be unfair to say that all employers make these kinds of judgments. Many go to great lengths to ensure that the selection process does not allow for discrimination. For the rest, you have an important part to play in the education process, but make sure you stay positive.

Healthy Eating

It is now generally accepted that a good diet is linked to robust health, with poor eating habits linked to a range of illnesses. It can sometimes take years for the effects to show themselves in the form of disease, but the good news is that for most of us it's comparatively easy to switch to a healthier style of eating.

In general, you should aim to eat a variety of foods, in sensible proportions. Ultimately, like exercise, diet is a personal matter, but following a few simple guidelines should put you on the right track:

- eat fewer fatty and sugary foods
- eat fresh fish and lean meat in preference to sausages and burgers
- stew or grill food in preference to frying in fat
- cut down on processed foods
- increase your intake of fibre-rich foods, like grains, fruits and vegetables
- limit the quantity of salt you take
- cut down on stimulants, such as coffee and alcohol
- eat three meals a day
- don't skip breakfast; it boosts your energy after a night's sleep and gets you off to a good start for the day

Fat should not be entirely eliminated from the diet, but medical research and population studies support the theory that a high intake of the *saturated* variety increases blood cholesterol levels and the risk of heart disease. Experts therefore recommend that we cut down on the foods that contain it, like fatty cuts of meat, butter and hard cheese. The same applies to *trans fats* which occur in hardened versions, such as margarine and lard. Watch out, too, for cakes, biscuits, pies and pastries, which often contain large hidden quantities of both kinds.

Think about your own diet. Is there anything you need to change?

Slimming

Every January a barrage of diet books hits the shops, promising easy and fun ways to lose weight. Most of us have indulged in one of these at some point, or at least skimmed through the pages, hoping that at last we will find the ultimate formula for painless slimming. These methods may well work for you, but if like many people you soon fall by the wayside, try going back to basics.

- Stick to a healthy and nourishing diet that suits your lifestyle and medical history, but reduce your calorie intake for a while. This means cutting down on confectionery, cakes, biscuits and alcohol, and reducing fat and sugar intake. Meticulous calorie counting isn't necessary; just use your common sense.
- Starchy foods like bread, pasta and potatoes are no longer considered a problem in themselves, but don't take them with fat.
- Substitute fresh fruit for snacks between meals.
- Take it slowly and comfortably, and use exercise to speed up your metabolism and tone your muscles.
- Don't be obsessive; if you slip up now and then, forgive yourself and start again.
- Once you have reached the right weight for your height, stick to a healthy eating plan, but don't overdo the portions.

The Business Lunch

This easy and popular excuse for abandoning a diet really doesn't stand up to scrutiny. The rules for slimmers eating out are the same as above, with the addition of a few helpful tips.

- Cut out the roll and butter.
- Pasta and potatoes are all right, but don't take them with heavy sauces or fat.
- Allow yourself one glass of wine, then opt for mineral water.
- Avoid the sweet trolley and ask for some fresh fruit instead.

When you're trying to clinch a deal, it's very unlikely that you are really giving much attention to the taste of your food anyway, so what have you got to lose? Celebrations are different; use these to loosen up a little and indulge in some treats.

Awareness Exercise

One very effective way to avoid overeating and enjoy your meals more is to focus your attention on *how* you eat. Next time you have a meal or snack try the following.

> *Chew your food thoroughly; taste it, enjoy it. Take it slowly, and only eat as much as you need. When you've had enough, stop. If you're alone, don't do anything else while eating, but allow yourself to be centred in the moment.*

Making this exercise a habit will not only help you lose weight, but will reduce your stress levels as well.

Sleep

Sleep deprivation is the scourge of the modern age, and most of us are familiar with the experience of lying awake for hours fretting about what we've got to do in the morning.

Medical opinion on how much sleep we require varies. Some experts say we need at least eight hours a night, while others recommend a core of only five or six. However, if you are constantly feeling tired, and illness has been ruled out, chances are you are not getting enough of the right kind of sleep. The current thinking is that we need more of the deep, non-dreaming variety.

Sleeping pills are not a long-term solution because they don't address the source of the problem. So what can be done about it?

One of the main causes of sleeplessness is stress, so deep relaxation will certainly help. People new to mind-body techniques are often ashamed when they find themselves falling asleep during sessions. In fact, this is an encouraging sign, indicating that the mind and body are catching up on the deep rest they have been denied in the past. Although this rest is deeper and more refreshing than sleep itself, it can also have a regulating effect on sleep patterns.

Systematic exercise and a balanced diet also play their part in helping you to get a good night's rest, as do the following tips from doctors:

➡ Keep your bedroom for sleeping in, and don't leave work lying around.
➡ Get up and do something rather than lying awake worrying.
➡ Don't get up late at weekends; it interferes with your body clock.
➡ Don't exercise late at night.
➡ Take a warm bath before retiring.
➡ Choose a milky drink last thing before bedtime, rather than stimulants like coffee, tea or alcohol.

If you are a real insomniac, and none of the above works, see your doctor, who may be able to recommend a sleep disorders clinic.

Your Environment

Most of us spend so much time in buildings or cars that we often overlook the benefits of breathing fresh air in parks and the countryside.

Escaping from built-up areas and traffic fumes on a regular basis should be a must for all urban dwellers. Natural light, grass, trees and flowers all relieve visual stress, allow us to breathe properly and cultivate a more harmonious approach to life.

That bright light alters the chemistry of the brain is very evident in sufferers from Seasonal Affective Disorder. As soon as the days shorten, their mood alters for the worse, and they can be plunged into depression. Fortunately, exposure to strong light has proved to be an effective therapy, although no one really knows how or why.

Although experiments and therapies use artificial light, nothing can beat the natural variety. Try getting out as often as possible to green, open spaces and see what a difference it makes to your sense of well-being.

Experiment, too, with bringing plants into your home and workplace. Not only do they add colour, but scientists have proved they're good for you. Researchers at the National Air and Space Association (NASA) found that rooms with plants have cleaner air, with one spider plant alone removing 96 per cent of carbon dioxide from a room used in the study.

Escape From Your Desk

If you are in a sedentary job, make sure you have regular breaks from what you are doing. Get up and stretch your legs and arms on a regular basis. This is even more important when you are sitting in front of a computer screen all day. Watch your posture and make sure your chair is the right height for your desk. If possible, get some fresh air at lunchtime, and don't be tempted to skip taking a food break if you have a lot to do. This might seem like a good idea at the time, but it will drain your energy and affect the quality of your work.

Corporate Help

So far we have focused on how you can help yourself healthwise, but you should also keep in mind what organizations are doing on their workers' behalf. For instance, if you are negotiating remuneration with a prospective employer, company health care insurance can play an important part in assessing the overall value of the benefits you receive. This may not be an obvious priority when you are young, but as you mature, you will find that good health can no longer be taken for granted. A good company scheme can pay dividends in terms of cash and peace of mind.

Organizations are beginning to wake up in a big way to the value of keeping their workforce fit, with some even providing on-site gyms or subsidizing health club memberships. No surprise then that the World Health Organization estimates that fitness and health issues will be central to the workplace culture in the millennium.

This should not encourage you to become complacent. Remember, you can no longer rely on steady employment with one company, and self-employment will become far more common in the years to come. Thinking ahead by researching independent provision makes very good economic sense.

An Holistic Approach

Taking an holistic approach to your well-being means taking care of yourself physically, mentally and spiritually. 'Spiritually' is a word usually associated with religion, but I use it in the broader sense of having an understanding of your inner energies as outlined in previous chapters. If you attend to this aspect of your being, then you are unlikely to become obsessive about exercise or dieting, and you will find following a balanced health plan is much easier. It also means there is no reason why vitality and strength should be confined to the young.

Making it Happen

Understanding the rules about good health won't in itself bring about changes. For that you will need a stimulus, so I suggest you write yourself an IOU. Write it boldly, and stick it up in a place where you will see it as an everyday reminder to be faithful to both your stress- and health-management plans.

I Owe Myself:

Inward nourishment from a healthy eating plan
Outward fitness from regular exercise
Underlying harmony from deep relaxation techniques

If you're wondering where you will find the time for all this, don't worry. The next chapter is devoted to that subject.

In the meantime, the chart below will help you to get started. When you have completed an action, make sure you make a note of the date. You will see the importance of this when you come to time management.

Option	Date	Estimated Expenditure
Investigate a medical check-up		
Visit a health club		
Research a personal fitness trainer		
Outline a regular exercise programme		
Draw up a healthy eating plan		

Don't forget to consult your doctor if you have any known medical problems or doubts about changing your routine.

SUMMARY

* Keeping fit and healthy gives you a competitive edge in the promotion and job search stakes.
* Good health includes not only physical fitness, but other lifestyle factors, like diet and stress management.

* Regular health check-ups are a good investment for the future.
* Effective physical exercise can range from walking to working out with a personal fitness trainer.
* Stay motivated by taking an holistic approach to your overall well-being.

Chapter Four

Time to Prosper

Setting positive goals is the
number one priority in getting
what you want out of life.

*'Must be able to meet challenging targets and work to tight dead-
lines.'* These personal qualities have long been a requirement in
sales jobs, but they are fast becoming standard across the professions. The pursuit of maximum productivity in the shortest possible time is now at the heart of business culture. Hence the popularity of time management courses.

Employers encourage their staff to develop time management
skills for the simple reason that more time means more profit. But
the rewards are not confined to companies. These skills also give
individuals the opportunity to breathe new life into personal and
professional ambitions. As you will see in Part Two, successfully
managing your own career is heavily dependent on how you
organize your time.

So what does time management involve? Clearly, we have no power
over time itself, so once again the real issue is *self*-transformation. It
is essentially about organizing yourself and your activities to:

➡ Optimize your energy levels
➡ Achieve your ambitions
➡ Boost your productivity

It is not about cramming as much as possible into every minute of
the day. On the contrary, you should be able to arrange your
schedule so that there is time for work and play, activity and rest.
Using time management in this way will help you to balance the

attainment of material prosperity with a happy and fulfilled personal life.

In fact, as soon as you embark on a structured stress and health management plan, you start to get the best out of your time. Paying attention to your well-being produces spontaneous, but noticeable benefits including:

⇒ improved quality of output
⇒ fewer mistakes
⇒ less time off work
⇒ more effective job-search strategies
⇒ more harmonious relationships
⇒ higher levels of motivation

But now it's time to go a step further, and learn how to create more space for the things that are important to you and the people who use your services.

Although the effects can be profound, the process itself is not complicated. Like any other form of expertise, time management takes determination at first, but with practice it will become an invaluable part of your regular routine. The five key elements are:

1. setting goals
2. prioritizing
3. combating information overload
4. time tracking
5. experiencing timeless awareness

Once you get to grips with these, you will have a framework to support all your efforts, whether at home or at work.

Setting Goals

Setting positive goals is the number one priority in getting what you want out of life. After all, organizations don't leave their profits to chance. They make forecasts of future performance, work to structured business plans, and establish measurement systems to ensure they stay on target. Although it may sound like a lot of effort, working to a plan makes their task a lot easier. The same goes for you. How can you achieve anything if you don't have a clear idea of what you're aiming for?

For example, you have already been given a lot of information about how to transform your life, but have you done anything to turn what you've read into knowledge? Remember, real knowledge comes from evaluation and practice. It's dynamic, not a passive absorption of facts.

Whatever you have or haven't done, have a go at setting a goal now, by writing down one small, achievable thing that you would like to accomplish over the next seven days. No matter how modest the task, it still constitutes a goal because it involves attainment of a desired outcome. Choose whatever you like, from making that business call you've been putting off for ages, to booking a meditation session. However, you must be *specific*, both in terms of the task itself and *when* you aim to complete it. Take some time out to think, then write it down.

Goal	Due by (date)	Completed (date)

If you achieve your goal on or before the due date, congratulate yourself. Setting a target date for a task reinforces your commitment to getting it done, and filling in the completion date gives you a sense of achievement. It will also encourage you to apply yourself to more substantial undertakings. Big successes are only the sum of a series of smaller ones.

Don't avoid challenging targets, but keep them within the bounds of what is reasonable within the time allocated. Likewise, your efforts won't last long unless you can measure your progress. Promising yourself more exercise is too vague, whereas aiming to be swimming twenty lengths a week by the end of next month gives you something quantifiable and easy to monitor. If the original target proves over- or under-ambitious, you are always free to adjust it.

Once you understand the basic principles, they can be put to work on more complex ambitions. The golden rule is to start with a main goal, then break it down into smaller steps. Let's say that moving to a larger house would make you happier. This would be your main goal; then you would look at what you *need* to get you there, like:

- making and saving some money
- identifying a new property
- selling your existing home

Each of these elements would then be broken down into even smaller, manageable chunks.

The same rule applies to career goals. Take the example of someone who wants to move into management. This major goal would be split into a series of timed, *enabling* actions such as:

- doing an audit of existing skills
- identifying opportunities
- getting any further qualifications

However, you should take care not to look at professional goals in isolation. Make sure they take their place within your overall personal aspirations. You can't go far wrong if you think first about how you want your *life* to look in the future, then decide where your career fits in. So many people do it the other way around, leading to all the stress associated with identifying too closely with their job. You will find more specific guidance about this in Chapter Eight.

Life Goals Exercise

Schedule a slot for some quiet time, then have a go at deciding how you would like your *life* to be in a few years' time. A four-year projection usually works well, but choose a longer or shorter period if you prefer. Planning significant changes seems daunting at first, so use the 3 Rs approach to keep stress at bay. Remember the rules:

- Relax
- Refresh
- Resume

By using a deep relaxation technique prior to goal-setting, you also set your intuition and creativity to work on your desires. To make the most of this, don't go straight for well-defined, rigid targets, but allow the ideas to flow, recording them randomly as they come. Organizing and refining is the second stage.

Asking yourself the following questions will help the visualization process:

Where am I?
What am I doing?
How do I feel?
Who else is in my life?

Jot down your thoughts on a piece of paper or wall chart. If it helps, draw pictures as well. Then summarize your ideas into a precise statement. Write or type it in bold letters on a single sheet of paper. This will be your *primary* goal, which can then be split into a series of enabling actions, which themselves can be subdivided, and so on. Never underestimate the power of writing things down; it has far more impact than simply keeping them in mind.

If you find yourself faced with the totally unexpected, take consolation from the fact that you are not alone. Let me give you two examples.

Jane wanted to smooth her path into management by organizing her diary more effectively. However, when it came to the life-planning exercise, her primary goal turned out to be 'Being in a steady relationship with a loving partner.' Nothing could have been further from her mind when she first walked through the door. The net result was not that she gave up her career ambitions, but that she took steps to balance this with making more time for social activities.

Mike, a salesman, was surprised to find that the main thing tying him to an unsuitable job was a reluctance to give up his company car. It was not until he clarified his life plans that he was able to recognize how trivial the problem was. Weighed against the fact that he was seeing less and less of his wife and child, the company vehicle suddenly paled into insignificance. The car in itself had not been the main obstacle. What Mike found difficult to relinquish was the symbol of success it represented. In fact, he was perfectly capable of repeating this success. His skills were transferable into a number of other professions, even if it did mean buying his own car in the short term.

These are not isolated cases, and I find that the personal relationship issue crops up time and again, often lying well hidden behind more superficial desires. This is not to say that someone who finds their plans dominated by career ambitions necessarily has a problem. Some people are able to pursue work that brings them great fulfilment, and they are happy to make it the main focus of their life. The important thing is knowing how to weigh up the issues before committing to any long-term plans.

Of course, this type of self-scrutiny may release feelings of vulnerability, which is why the 3 Rs play such an important part. Fortunately, identifying the smaller, *enabling* goals is much easier. This is because they usually involve more immediate action, rather than soul searching. In the process, they also transform fear into energy, which makes them excellent stress busters.

Goals at Work

So far we have looked at self-generated aims, but, of course, there will also be a great many demands imposed on you by others. This is particularly true at work, where you will sometimes have very little control over what you are expected to do. In theory, the company should provide a job description and a set of mutually agreed objectives, with your performance regularly measured against predetermined criteria. In this ideal world, your manager's door is always open, and your annual assessment throws up no surprises.

Sadly, reality often falls far short of the theory. Managers inhabit the same erratic universe as the rest of us, and who can blame them if they don't always conform to the ideal? As a result, you may find yourself becoming task-driven, with no clear idea of where you fit into the overall plan. The problem is compounded if you are working in temporary or contract employment.

Resolving issues like this can be difficult, and the danger is that you will become demotivated and resentful in the meantime. One powerful solution is to draw up your own objectives and performance criteria. Every time you clock up a successful outcome, you are reinforcing a belief in yourself as a winner. If your ingenuity doesn't impress the boss, make plans to find an organization where your independence and energy will be appreciated.

Prioritizing

Have you ever noticed how successful people have an uncanny knack of homing in on the key issues, and getting straight to the heart of a problem? They are not necessarily the most talented, or even the most hard-working, but what they do have is the ability to *prioritize* effectively. This is why they are able to handle such large workloads, and cope admirably with a variety of projects, while others struggle to keep their heads above water with far fewer responsibilities. Some individuals are naturally gifted in this way, but the good news is that it is a skill that can be learned by anyone.

Prioritizing is about distinguishing between the important and the unimportant, and reacting accordingly. This is not as easy as it sounds, which is why well-organized business people tend to use structured systems to filter and categorize their responsibilities before deciding how to handle them.

Let's examine one of these methods, starting with the relatively simple example of prioritizing a 'to do' list. You may have one of these already, and no doubt the prospect of ticking off the items one by one is very satisfying. But the chances are you are dealing with the easy tasks first, and this is not an effective use of time. To make a list work, each task needs to be prioritized and tackled according to its importance.

If you don't have one already, make a list below:

Things to Do
....
....
....
....
....
....
....
....
....
....

Now go back to the list and prioritize the tasks. Try grouping them as follows:

> A – Highest importance
> B – Important, but can wait for now
> C – May not be necessary; revisit
> D – Unimportant; scrap

They can then be broken down further into A1, A2, and so on. If in doubt about what's important, ask yourself:

> does this contribute to my goals?
> can someone else do it?
> what will happen if I don't do it?

Then go back and assign each item a 'due' and 'completed' date. Be ready to revisit your list and change the priorities if necessary. If this method doesn't appeal to you, invent your own. Whatever system you use, be ruthless with unimportant items; don't leave them hanging around to play on your mind.

Once you are familiar with the basic rules, exactly the same method can be applied to your other endeavours. The success of any major project will depend on your ability to subdivide it into smaller, prioritized tasks.

Combating information overload

At this stage, on business courses, participants used to be asked to prioritize a simulated 'in-basket', with duties ranging from answering memos to making phone calls. However, the days of the traditional in-basket are numbered, and we are now faced with an altogether more lethal beast, largely driven by the revolution in electronic communications. This has produced a phenomenon known as 'information overload', something that is threatening to spiral out of control in the 21st century.

This glut of facts not only wastes time, but can lead to high levels of stress. Because there is so much information around, often transmitted at the touch of a button, we are all expected to know more about everything, and make an instant response. What's more we feel obliged to absorb all sorts of unnecessary facts, if only to avoid relegation to the ranks of the information underclass.

The problem can be even worse for job hunters, who are often faced with a tantalizing but overwhelming choice of useful information. There are specific tips on this in Chapter Ten, but to make the most of them, you will first need to absorb the general guidance in this section.

Clearly, something has to be done about all this. For executives and senior management, one remedy is to pay someone else to absorb the facts and come up with summarized reports. Keep this in mind for the future, but what can you do right now?

Fortunately, information can be filtered in the same way that a list is prioritized. Despite the wizardry of new technology, we are far from achieving the paperless office, so let's start with incoming hard copy mail. Sort this into folders marked 'Action' or 'Read', and confine anything unimportant to the waste bin.

Set aside specific times for reading, and stick to them. Be innovative about creating reading opportunities; for instance, might it sometimes be better to leave your car at home and travel by train or take a flight? Make the most of periods when you are forced to sit waiting for customers or the boss. Scanning is also a good way to speed up your reading. Apply yourself first to the opening and closing paragraphs of any item to register the central message in your brain, then go back and scan the rest.

Now for the difficult part. Used properly, electronic communications can only make our lives easier, but not when they become a burden. Obsession with the Internet and the World Wide Web has come to present a unique threat to our productivity. Sending and responding to e-mail often becomes a priority, for no other reason than that it all happens at the click of the mouse. Add to that the temptation to trawl for all manner of fascinating, but often useless, information, and we become trapped in a downward spiral.

The secret of mastering this monster is rigid self-discipline. You must apply all the rules you have already learned, plus:

➡ Use software designed to help you prioritize e-mail and create electronic 'to do' lists.
➡ Limit your use of the Internet to specific times of the day.
➡ Don't encourage junk mail by giving out your e-mail address to all and sundry.
➡ Ask people to be disciplined in what they send, and return the courtesy.
➡ Think before you print out voluminous reports and newsletters.
➡ Keep on top of technology by retraining where necessary.

Approached in this way, technology ceases to rule our lives, and reverts to being the productivity tool it was originally designed to be.

You may not yet be a victim, but information overload is destined to be one of the biggest time and stress management issues of the next century, so make sure you know how to deal with it in advance.

Time Tracking

Once you have decided on your priorities, and have some firm goals in place, you will be ready to put your overall use of time under scrutiny. As well as helping you to measure your progress, this exercise will also highlight any time-wasting habits.

First, make sure your diary entries are up-to-date for the next seven consecutive days. If these are not typical, then choose other days. Include work and leisure, and use separate diaries if necessary. Next, take seven photocopies of the Time Tracker sheet at the end of this chapter (one for each day), and use them to record brief notes of your activities, preferably as you go along.

To get the maximum benefit out of this exercise, you will need to analyse the results carefully and be totally honest with yourself. Use the following to help you decide what to look for:

➡ how do my activities measure up to my diary forecasts?
➡ how much of my time is devoted to achieving my goals?
➡ how many time-wasters can I identify?
➡ am I devoting enough time to my mental and physical well-being?
➡ do I achieve a balance between work and play, activity and rest?
➡ am I paying enough attention to my finances?
➡ do I leave enough contingency time to cope with the unexpected?

Most people are surprised to discover how they spend their time, especially when they view their performance in the light of the 80/20 rule. This rule, first defined in the 19th century, states that 80 per cent of what we achieve comes from 20 per cent of the time and effort we expend. This means you will almost certainly find plenty of room for improvement in how you focus your efforts. Lack of planning is the main reason why so much energy is expended on simply maintaining the status quo, rather than moving forward.

Working out an action plan may be a substantial undertaking, so take it little by little. We have already examined some substantial time-wasters, such as failure to set goals and undisciplined use of the Internet, but you will no doubt find many others to work on. The following are some commonly identified culprits:

Clutter is a major problem at home and at work, so treat yourself to a clear-out as soon as possible. Tackle everything, from filing systems to your wardrobe. Throw out what you don't need, and make sure everything else is in its place. If it doesn't have a place, make one. Getting rid of rubbish and organizing your surroundings creates space, which in turn brings energy. You will also regain a sense of control, and be less likely to put things off.

The telephone can be a nightmare if not used properly, so train yourself to be disciplined in making and receiving calls. Don't be afraid to screen calls by using an answer-machine or equipment that displays the caller's number. Keep your business conversations focused by preparing what you want to say in advance, and have a good excuse ready to wind up if the other side gets too talkative. Mobile phones are a mixed blessing, so use them with caution, and only give your number to those with a real need to know.

Business travel requires innovative planning. For instance, aim to accomplish as many meetings as possible in one trip, rescheduling them if necessary. On the plus side, as we have seen, some journeys actually present an opportunity to save time by catching up on reading. This is equally true of report writing and other tasks. You can also use hotel leisure centres to help you keep fit.

Working from home may not yet be a major part of your schedule, but be prepared to face up to it in the future. Being at home should make life a lot easier, but it often has the reverse effect, presenting a host of reasons not to get started or indulge in pleasant interruptions. To overcome this, try to create working space away from your normal areas of activity, and shake off the cobwebs by going for an early morning walk or getting some exercise. Stick to scheduled hours so that your work does not spill over into rest and leisure periods.

In reality, there is no end to the things that may constitute a time-waster, just as there is no limit to what may generate stress. In fact, everything that causes stress is also a time-waster, so your stress management plan will play an important role in tackling your time management issues. Negative behavioural traits deserve particular attention, so don't leave them out of the equation. *Procrastination* is the greatest enemy of initiative, and should be at the top of your hit list.

Make a note here of the main factors you have identified as barriers to your progress:

The final step is to turn the above into measurable goals. For instance, if you find that lack of funds is preventing you from getting what you want, don't waste time fretting about it. Instead, put your energy into drawing up a personal budget plan, listing all your income, then all of your likely spending. When you know exactly how much you have to live on, it will be much easier to prioritize your outgoings and make plans to save. The same goes for clearing debt; take the stress out of the situation by setting targets for clearing it, no matter how small the repayments may be.

In fact, money looms large in most people's minds, so it will almost certainly be a feature of your action plan. Remember, too, that continuity of income will not be guaranteed in the workplace of the future, so from now on make the most of the good times by investing for leaner periods. Think of money as a potent form of energy, and treat it with the same respect you accord to your health. Financial fitness means not letting your resources get lazy, so make it a point to shop around for the best deals in pensions, savings and insurance.

Once you have a plan of attack, there is no need to repeat the time tracking exercise in such detail, or it will defeat the object and become a time waster in itself. What you need above all is a firm commitment to change. Once you have this, you will find it much easier to monitor yourself.

Experiencing Timeless Awareness

Understanding the benefits of timeless awareness will give you a unique advantage in the time management stakes.

Many people stay within time-bound consciousness throughout their waking hours, and this starves them of the opportunity to access that state of awareness where time has no power. Our experience of time comes from our thoughts, but when we allow these to quieten down, our minds and bodies follow, bringing deep rest and renewed vitality. If you are already practising deep relaxation techniques on a regular basis, you will know the truth of this.

Where there is no time, there is no fear. Problems exist in time, but, as we saw in Chapter One, when you leave this behind for a while, your hunches and intuition come to the fore. This adds another dimension to your decision making and speeds up your ability to prioritize.

Taking the Helm

Systematically working towards your own targets will give you a sense of control over your destiny, despite the turbulent times ahead. It will also foster a growth towards independence, which will sustain you through any gaps in employment.

Employers and service users want people who are results-oriented. Making goals and priorities a part of your daily routine will help you to speak their language. Being able to speak with ease about your achievements and how you organize yourself is guaranteed to make you stand out from the crowd, especially when you are faced with an interview.

Overall, you may be exhilarated by the speed at which you can change your circumstances, but don't be surprised if you also feel tired at the outset, particularly if you are facing up to issues that have lain dormant for years. This is one reason why you should always keep your plans flexible.

Life has a habit of presenting us with a variety of unforeseen obstacles, so accept that things won't always go your way. Once again, *action* is the best possible antidote to disappointment. Aim for balance, and stick to the 3 Rs. Remember, too, that there may be consequences for those around you, so make sure your plans take account of their needs.

Of course, organizing yourself effectively does not solve the dilemma of the truly impossible targets and unrealistic deadlines you may face at work. This is essentially a communications challenge, demanding sound interpersonal skills, the subject of the next chapter.

SUMMARY

* Time management is about organizing yourself and your activities to achieve your ambitions and boost your productivity.
* Setting goals and prioritizing tasks and activities creates space for the things that are important to you and the people who use your services.
* Career ambitions should take their due place within your overall aims.

TIME TRACKER

Day: *Date:*

8.00	1.00
9.00	2.00
10.00	3.00
11.00	4.00
12.00	5.00 onwards

* Every time you register a successful outcome, you are reinforcing a belief in yourself as a winner.
* Effective time management means being results-oriented, a quality that is guaranteed to impress bosses and recruiters.

Chapter Five

Warrior in the Workplace

Qualifications and professional
aptitude count for little if you do
not develop political awareness.

The Importance of People

Job seekers are often euphoric when they land the job of their
dreams. In some cases this turns out to be justified, but there are
others who find themselves unprepared for the more treacherous
elements of corporate culture.

Years of recession and uncertainty have created an environment where people are often afraid to speak up for themselves in
case they lose their jobs. Many temporary and contract workers
are accustomed to being treated as second-class citizens, but even
permanent staff frequently face the prospect of intimidation by
jealous colleagues or bullying bosses. In this climate, the workplace can resemble a battlefield, where only the seasoned warriors are able to stay the course. If you are going to survive, it
makes sense to follow their lead, and learn something about the
art of warfare.

This is a battle of wits, rather than physical combat, and victory will depend on how much support you are able to muster
from those around you. Get it wrong and you will find that other
people can ruin all your carefully laid plans and reduce your
nerves to pulp. They can make outrageous demands, turn your
priorities upside down, and make your life hell.

On the other hand, people are your only route to success.
Everything you achieve in life is in some way attributable to your
past or present relationships with other people. Think about it.

What have you ever accomplished without someone else to lend a hand or inspire you at some stage in the proceedings? Your helpers will have appeared in many different guises, from parents and teachers, to friends and managers.

Even when you work for yourself, success depends on having someone to buy your goods or services and supply your materials. Whoever they are, superiors, colleagues or customers, other people have a considerable degree of power over your future. Whether they prove a hindrance or a help is largely a matter of your own powers of observation and persuasion.

Ultimately, you cannot control others or how they behave, but you can learn to *influence* them in your favour. This means developing strong interpersonal skills and being able to hold your nerve when obstacles are put in your way. These qualities are important in all walks of life, but never more so than in the new world of work.

The Battlefield

As we have seen, a great many people spend their lives defending their ego. At work this often takes the form of power play, commonly known as 'politics', which is simply warfare by another name. At one level this type of activity stems from frustration and disappointment, and may show itself as sullenness and lack of cooperation. At the other extreme, we have the skilled manipulator, a far more deadly animal. This is the character who thrives on adversity, is a sublime strategist, and an expert in creating and exploiting dissent for his or her own ends.

In some cases, perfectly capable people are frozen out of jobs without ever discovering why, which is exactly what happened to Danielle, an experienced administrator with a business-related degree. At first she was overjoyed to find a position with an organization renowned for its staff training and promotion policies, where she would be supporting board members and interacting with executive customers. This, she thought, would give her valuable exposure to the decision makers, and mark a turning point in her career. Sadly, nothing could have been further from the truth.

No matter how hard she tried, the two established members of the team refused to accept her into the fold. Her mistreatment was subtle, but effective. Essential information was withheld, she was confined to junior duties, and verbal communications remained strained. Danielle struggled on for three weary months, then gave up the battle.

The most likely explanation was that Danielle's qualifications and evident talent presented a threat to her colleagues, and their solution was to label her as the 'enemy'. For Danielle's part, although she had devoted a great deal of time and effort to getting vocational training, she had only a rudimentary grasp of assertiveness techniques. She was also too slow in taking the problem up the line when her own efforts failed. By the time Personnel were in the picture, she had already resolved to leave.

Although this particular case involves a woman, I have also encountered a significant number of men who have suffered a similar fate. In a male environment, the language may be cruder and the tactics more brutal, but the principle is the same. Qualifications and professional aptitude count for little if you do not develop political awareness.

The higher you climb, the more sophisticated the game becomes. In this environment, when alliances are formed and enemies identified, you may find yourself perceived as being in one camp or another, whatever the reality of the situation. This is where a personal survival strategy is essential.

The most important thing to know is that the instigators of malicious campaigns are bullies, and bullies are *always* motivated by fear and insecurity. If you decide to play the game their way, the price you pay is loss of integrity and inner harmony. Not only that, if you possess any degree of insight, you are unlikely to win if you accept their terms of engagement. People who devote their whole being to trampling on others can be extremely good at it, so, although you should stay alert to their scheming, your best chance of competing is to develop an approach which is entirely out of their experience.

Fortunately, there are more noble combatants to model yourself on. These are the individuals who accept that competition is essential to business success, but are able to engage in manoeuvres with panache and style. They have a healthy sense of team spirit, and work towards goals without personalizing issues or building resentment. They also recognize that strong team players will be the winners of the future, where the trend will be for people to come together for specific projects, then reband into different groups or move on to other organizations. This pattern of working requires the ability to fit in quickly, leaving little room for prima donnas or disruptive types.

Following their example takes considerable strength of character, but it should be within your range, particularly if you are able to combine contemporary personal effectiveness techniques with the wisdom of time-tested systems.

'War' is a word associated with brutality and bloodshed, but when you are well prepared there is no need to be destructive. On the contrary, your weapons will be:

➡ inner knowledge and strength
➡ an understanding of what motivates others
➡ a sound grasp of assertiveness and negotiating techniques
➡ an insight into political manoeuvring and competitive strategies

Psychological Preparation

> *The greatest warrior is the one who conquers himself.*
>
> SAMURAI TEACHING

Your success in battle depends to a large extent on how well you are able to prepare yourself mentally. We saw in Chapter One that the Tao Te Ching can act as a resource for personal growth, but the martial arts, which owe much of their philosophy to

Taoist teachings, have an even more direct relevance to the modern-day warrior.

In ancient China it was believed that success in warfare depended on the development of mental abilities that encompassed a philosophical and spiritual dimension. When these teachings were transported to Japan, they were evolved into the Zen martial arts. The underlying philosophy has endured and is still central to modern sports like kendo and judo.

The masters of these sports strive to achieve a complete unity of mind, body and spirit, which takes them out of the arena of mere aggression or defensiveness. This is no whimsical ideology, but a practical approach that has been put to the test by Western scientists.

In one physiological experiment, a Kendo master, who used meditation as part of his preparation, was wired up to an electrocardiogram to test his heart rate over four practice sessions with a less experienced opponent of similar age and fitness. Despite intense physical activity, the master's heart rate was found to be consistently lower than his opponent's, which would be consistent with a calmer mental state throughout.

This is just one example of how scientists are studying sports people to understand how mind-body techniques seem to give them a competitive advantage. However, with regular practice of deep relaxation, we can all experience this for ourselves, and substantially increase our chance of winning on the battlefield at work.

Before we leave the subject, there is one further success factor to consider. This is a phenomenon known to the Japanese as *mushin*, which translates as 'no-mind' or 'without thinking'. It entails clearing the mind of extraneous thoughts and concentrating on a single aim such as 'I will win'. The idea is that the game and player become one, and the individual spontaneously makes the right moves.

Exercise

Clearly this type of mental preparation has a lot to offer the workplace warrior, who needs to prepare for different, but equally challenging, confrontations. Next time you get warning of a confrontation at work, try using the same type of auto-suggestion to get yourself into a winning frame of mind:

1. Use your preferred mind-body technique to reach a state of deep relaxation.
2. Allow yourself the usual time to experience inner calm.
3. As you start to resurface, imagine yourself going through the confrontation and coming out as the winner. Let yourself feel good about the outcome.

If you look a little closer, this is just a slight variation on the goal-setting exercise in the last chapter. Not surprisingly, visualization is becoming a very popular element of management development courses, but it is something anyone can do. Using a mind-body technique as the first stage will also give you a considerable advantage. It is at the point of transition, between the state of profound relaxation and waking consciousness, that your thoughts are at their most powerful. Making your suggestion at this stage gives you the best possible chance of firmly rooting a belief in your ability to succeed.

The very act of regarding yourself as a warrior brings a great deal of energy. This simple shift of focus can help you to summon courage in many situations that would normally send you running for cover.

Asserting Yourself

Once you have established the right mind-set, the next step is to look at how you can become more assertive in your dealings with the people around you. This will enhance your communication skills by helping you to speak up for yourself without trampling on others. Although assertiveness training is a thoroughly modern concept, in emphasizing self-awareness and balance, it has many parallels with the teachings of the Tao and other ancient traditions. Taken together they offer a potent formula for success.

To understand how assertive behaviour can help you, it is important to appreciate the difference between this and other types of behaviour. Broadly speaking, the way we operate can be divided into three categories. Tick the description that most closely resembles your current behaviour in challenging situations:

Aggressive behaviour is where we press our point regardless of the views of others. This makes us appear pushy and overbearing.

Non-assertive or submissive behaviour is where we submit to others' views and needs at the expense of our own, often ending up feeling ignored and resentful.

Assertive behaviour is where we weigh our views against those of others. This allows us to make our point, while respecting the rights of colleagues.

Aggressive types often get what they want in the short term, but they are equally prone to lose out over longer periods of time. Resentment can sometimes build up slowly, but when it does, they may find themselves targeted when the time comes for corporate cuts.

Non-assertive characters tend to be all-round losers. In suppressing their needs, they can become angry and frustrated, leading to all manner of stress-related health problems. They are unlikely to do well at work, and are a prime target for bullies.

Most of us tend to use a mix of these behaviours, but usually one or the other will dominate. Adopting an assertive stance helps us to achieve a better balance, and makes it far easier to get what we want out of life.

So how is this achieved?

1. *Listen actively*

People tend to be surprised that listening is one of the most valuable of all interpersonal skills. We usually pay far more attention to what *we* are saying than what the other person is trying to put across. It may be quite natural, but it does not help when we want to persuade others to our cause. In future, make an effort to relax when you listen, so that you can give the speaker your full attention. Nod now and then, and summarize from time to time, to show that you have really grasped the message. Don't be afraid to ask for complex points to be repeated, but do it politely. The effect of these simple techniques can be remarkable. Active listening makes people feel valued, which in turn will motivate them to listen to your arguments.

2. Ask for what you want

Don't assume other people will always know what you want, then blame them for being insensitive. When you make a request be firm, but polite. Be direct, rather than apologizing for yourself. Non-assertive people are renowned for hesitant language, like, 'I'm sorry for being such a nuisance, but . . .' and 'I know you'll think this is ridiculous . . .' On the whole, people will treat you the way you expect to be treated. Don't set yourself up for a put-down.

3. Focus on the facts

When we are under pressure, it is easy to become emotional, especially when we face a confrontation. In these situations, resist the temptation to exchange insults or generalize. For instance, instead of saying, 'You are a useless time-keeper,' say, 'You have been late for the last two meetings; is there a problem?' This gives the other party a chance to explain without losing face. Likewise, when opponents hurl insults at you, steer them back to the facts.

4. Allow others to let off steam

Mark, a customer service manager, is accustomed to dealing with complaints from the public. By the time callers have got to him, they have often been passed from pillar to post and are in a state of total frustration. 'I always let them have their say,' he said. 'Once they've thoroughly vented their spleen, they usually calm down a bit. Then I sympathize with them, which takes them off their guard, and gives me the advantage. After that it's usually easy to establish a rapport and sort the matter out.' Try this next time someone loses their temper with you.

5. *Practise saying 'No'*

Many of us are taught from childhood that pleasing other people is paramount. As a result, we can find ourselves giving in to others, even when our inner voice is screaming 'no'. Let's say you have been asked to stay late at work when you have made arrangements to go to a show with your partner. Don't just say 'no', but explain the situation calmly without being over-apologetic. However, don't leave it at that. Let the boss know you realize how important the work is, and discuss other ways of getting it done.

6. *Match your body language to the situation*

The success of all the above techniques depends to a large extent on the body language you use. For instance, how you hold yourself and the tone of voice you use should match the situation. It's pointless saying 'no' to the boss if you hunch your shoulders and avoid eye contact. On the other hand, if the person confronting you is looking vulnerable and hurt, it may pay to soften your voice and adopt a sympathetic stance.

The last point to remember, before we move on to other techniques, is that over-attachment to ego is your greatest enemy. When you are able to let go of this, you have already won the greatest part of the battle. Only by regularly dipping into your deeper consciousness will you be able to ensure that your perceptions remain unclouded by your own prejudices and projections. This clarity of vision will also give you the power to watch for your opponents' real strengths and weaknesses, rather than the illusions they will try to create for your benefit.

Negotiating

Negotiating techniques take the benefits of assertiveness a stage further in the range of bargaining strategies. Although the formal variety can be complex, a grasp of the basics should be enough to help you in your everyday dealings with colleagues and bosses. The same goes for transactions with interviewers, employment agencies or any other organization that wants to buy your skills or services.

When you enter any discussion with the aim of coming to an agreement, stick to the following guidelines and you can't go far wrong:

- prepare your case thoroughly
- believe in the value of what you have to 'sell'
- get your timing right
- see the issue from both sides
- allow room for manoeuvre
- aim for a win/win situation

Let's take the example of asking for a pay rise. As a marketing manager, Ellen is no amateur when it comes to negotiating with customers. However, she thought it wise to rehearse her strategy with me before asking her boss for a substantial salary increase. Her initial plan was to base her request on an advertisement for a similar, but better paid, position in the industry. Even as we talked, she began to realize that on its own this might be a rash approach. What if he called her bluff and asked her to apply for the other job? In the event, she changed her tactics, and got the 25 per cent increase she wanted.

So how was it done?

- Ellen took the time to sit down and write out every major achievement since her last pay rise, showing the precise benefits to the company in terms of increased market share and financial profit.
- She timed her move to coincide with the successful conclusion of a major event she had organized, putting herself in the best possible bargaining position.

- She started by asking her boss for a performance review, rather than a pay rise, which might have encouraged him to take a confrontational stance.
- She asked him to evaluate her performance, occasionally helping out by consulting her prepared list. This produced a positive response, and led smoothly into a salary discussion.
- She asked for a higher amount than she actually expected, thus allowing the boss room to manoeuvre.

This approach allowed the boss to feel in control at all times, and totally avoided any conflict. Ellen was delighted with the ease of her success.

> 'I didn't even realize myself how much I'd achieved until I wrote it all down. That's why I felt so confident throughout the meeting. I've also noticed that my ideas get much more air time these days.'

Asking for something is one reason for using negotiating techniques, but they are equally useful when you want to avoid something. The impossible deadline is a classic example. In a stressful situation like this, don't surrender to panic. *This is the worst possible thing to do*. Once you calm down, you will see that there is nearly always room for negotiation, no matter how small. The key is to remember that the boss wants a *solution*, not a problem. Whatever the content, try to frame your message in a positive way, even if ultimately you are saying 'no'.

In this situation, there are several things you can do:

- check if anyone else can help
- work out if at least a part of the work can be done in the set time
- go back with a revised completion date

There's no guarantee that this will do the trick every time, but at least you will come out with more respect than if you respond with an emotional outburst. Staying positive also keeps your stress levels under control. If you find it keeps happening, first check your own time management, then don't delay in asking for a meeting to get to the bottom of the issue.

In other situations, *delay* may be just what's needed. Carl is an expert in the power of delay. His manager has the habit of calling impromptu meetings on a Friday afternoon to discuss major operational changes. Caught off their guard, most of the staff tend to go along with the suggestions, not least because they want to get off for the weekend. Carl wants to get away too, but he never rushes into an agreement. Instead, he adopts a thoughtful expression which shows how much he values the manager's ideas. Then he asks politely if he can get back to her in a few days' time, 'because it's far too important to rush into a decision'. By that time, of course, he has prepared a convincing case for doing things his own way. Carl's approach works every time, largely due to the warmth and charm that mask his will of iron.

Although you may not succeed in getting such positive outcomes at the first attempt, don't be discouraged by early failures. Keep positive by regarding your move as a preliminary attempt, and make notes of the plus and minus points to help you do better next time.

Learning from the Politicians

So far, we have dwelt on the negative aspects of political manoeuvring, but there is another side. At its best, political communication is about using advanced presentational skills to appeal to the widest possible audience. This positive aspect offers many useful lessons for the person who aspires to climb the career ladder.

Put this to the test next time a political debate or interview comes up on television. Resist the temptation to switch channels, and get out your notebook instead. Watch how the more appealing types get their message across by:

➡ paying attention to how they dress
➡ using positive body language
➡ varying their voice pitch
➡ employing memorable slogans and soundbites

- turning negatives into positives
- knowing when to be economical with the truth

This is the result of intensive training in presentation skills by spin doctors, PR consultants, voice trainers and a host of other experts. Business executives undergo similar intensive coaching to ensure they come across effectively.

The moral is that if you want to get on in business, pay attention to your image. Assertiveness and negotiating techniques will take you a long way, but getting to the top takes that bit more. So many ambitious people fall by the wayside because they fail to match vocational training with the skill of self-promotion.

Giving presentations and public speaking are no longer the preserve of people at the top. In this multimedia age, they are becoming common even in relatively junior positions. You may never face a television appearance, but video-conferencing of job interviews looks set to become commonplace in the millennium, and learning how to perform on camera will add another string to your bow.

Getting professional help is the best way to polish your image. If politicians can re-invent themselves so successfully with the help of consultants, so can you. If you are already working, check out if the company is willing to send you on a course. Use your negotiating powers to persuade them it will be to their advantage. If you are a student, there may be something on offer at your college or university. If there really is nothing available, set a goal to book your own course when finances allow. Evening classes tend to be an inexpensive option, at least to get you started.

The Art of Strategy

Returning to the warrior theme, it will also pay to study how executives attack strategic and competitive challenges. To get started, try reading a translation of Sun Tzu's military classic, *The Art of War*. Although written twenty-five centuries ago, in recent years it has become highly popular with management consultants and business schools, who recognize its value to contemporary situations.

Sun Tzu believed that victory comes long before the confrontation if the warrior is able to observe carefully and outmanoeuvre his adversary. This has obvious relevance to competitive business situations, which is why modern interpretations draw helpful parallels for the reader. One version you might like to consult is *Sun Tzu, the Art of War for Executives*, by Donald G. Krause, a work which combines the insights of the original with the ideas of contemporary business philosophers.

Know your Rights

No matter how well trained you are, there is always the possibility that somewhere in your career your will run into trouble.

Expect the best but prepare for the worst by checking the small print on your contract, and understanding exactly what your formal rights are. Don't leave it until you hit a rough patch; negotiate any changes while you are still in a position to do so.

If you get involved in an ongoing dispute, always keep step by step notes of what happens in case you need to defend yourself against an accuser. Take copies of any documentation that may prove relevant, including electronic communications.

Make a point of keeping abreast of changes in employment legislation, particularly laws dealing with discrimination. In the UK, legislation is strong on racial and sexual discrimination, weaker on disability, and totally absent where age is concerned. Americans are more fortunate, with strong measures to cover all four areas.

Going to court may be a last resort, but if the need arises, you may have to move quickly. There are often time limits on applying for help. But always keep this knowledge to yourself until you need it; nothing is guaranteed to infuriate an employer more than an amateur lawyer with an attitude.

If you find yourself facing the chop without a redundancy package or the benefit of outplacement (careers guidance offered by companies to those affected by redundancy), it's worth trying to negotiate a payment in kind. For instance, is the company prepared to let you use their premises and computer equipment to search for a new job?

If you are one of the many people in a non-permanent position, you may find yourself with no rights to compensation, but don't make assumptions; there are always exceptions, so check it out anyway.

If you are forced to leave your job, don't see this as a defeat. Staying in a situation that puts you under constant pressure is bad for your health, so getting out may be the best option. Even the most skilled warriors face setbacks, but they use the experience to go on to victory the next time round.

Performance Tracking

The techniques and strategies in this chapter will help you to transform your professional relationships and get the things you want, but change will not happen overnight. The most important thing now is to watch how you behave in certain situations, then make a note of what you did well or where you went wrong. Photocopy the Performance Tracker at the end of this chapter to help you do this.

Never push yourself too hard. Start with something easy, like active listening. Even small things can bring remarkable benefits. When you have clocked up a few successes, move on to more challenging techniques. Don't be afraid to ask for feedback from people you can trust. Even when you encounter hostile criticism, listen carefully; you may just learn something to your advantage. This is a key element in building a more positive outlook, which is why we shall look at it more closely in the next chapter.

Although we have concentrated largely on situations at work, the tactics discussed are every bit as relevant in a job search context; hostile and difficult characters are to be found everywhere, and you certainly can't afford to lose your cool with recruiters, government departments or agencies.

INCIDENT	HOW DID I HANDLE IT?	LEARNING POINTS FOR FUTURE

PERFORMANCE TRACKER

SUMMARY

* Knowledge of the art of war can pay dividends on the battlefields of work and during job searching.
* Political awareness, assertiveness and negotiating skills are central to survival.
* Watch the politicians to gain an insight into self-promotion strategies.
* Know your rights and always check the small print on your contract.
* Keep a log of how you perform in challenging situations to help you do better in the future.

Chapter Six

Positivity Pays

In modern times, everyone is
looking for the *feelgood* factor,
and the individual who delivers
this will reap the rewards
financially and emotionally.

Adding Value

'Added value' is a term used in marketing to sell products or services by offering benefits which go beyond standard expectations. It is a concept that can also be applied to your professional
image. We have already looked at many ways to add value to
your personal skills, but now we come to a quality that is often
overlooked in the rush for technical competence; the ability to
stay positive when the going gets tough.

Maggie has the magic touch. For her, there is no such thing as
an impossible situation. Whatever the problem, she takes an
upbeat approach and inspires others with her enthusiasm. This
makes her hugely popular with managers and colleagues, and she
is always the first to be invited on to the team when a new project
comes up.

To understand Maggie's popularity you need only put yourself
in the place of the people she works with. In these times of esca-
lating pressure, we all appreciate people who bring light and
energy into our working lives. Small wonder that individuals
with this ability are in such demand. If you want further evidence, just look through a selection of job advertisements and see
how often employers expect candidates to be 'enthusiastic' and
'highly motivated'. They are well aware that positivity has a

direct impact on the bottom line.

Of course, there is more than the employer's perspective to consider. There is also the matter of keeping yourself motivated through more frequent job changes in the millennium. This will entail a greater number of job applications, which in turn will bring the prospect of more rejections. If you allow this cycle of events to bring you down, your chances of success will be considerably eroded, and you will find your social diary empties as quickly as your business one.

This does not necessarily mean you will have to become the life and soul of the party. Maggie is a quiet person with no aspirations towards leadership. She is modest about her personal qualities, and attributes her success to always remembering that she has a choice about how she reacts to the world around her. Her personality has not changed, but self-discipline has considerably brightened her outlook over the years.

Some people have a naturally pleasant disposition, and thoroughly enjoy using techniques which can take them a step further. Others find the process more difficult, particularly if they are under a lot of stress. In this chapter we are going to look at a number of techniques that I have seen used to good effect by clients and other contacts. However, they are only options, not hard and fast rules, so feel free to choose or reject as you see fit. Take your time, and don't worry if some of the ideas seem a little challenging at this stage. You can always come back to them another time.

The techniques we will explore are:

➧ intercepting negative thoughts
➧ listing achievements
➧ learning from the entrepreneurs
➧ encouraging feedback
➧ giving constructive criticism

Intercepting Negative Thoughts

Anger and annoyance are natural reactions in stressful situations, but the real problem begins when negative tendencies start to dominate our outlook. This can happen with alarming speed when we face changes in our career or find ourselves out of work. However, it is something that must be addressed if we are to make progress professionally. For instance, it is essential to get yourself into a positive frame of mind before going for a job interview. Most interviewers will make allowances for nerves, but the slightest hint of negativity will set off alarm bells.

The first step in the process is to become aware of negative thoughts and limiting beliefs as they arise. At first you will have to make a conscious effort, but after a few weeks you should find the warning signals switching on automatically. This doesn't have to be a solemn exercise. The objective is not to make an in-depth inventory of all your problems, but just to see how easy it is to slip into a negative drift.

When I asked a group of clients to do this, they were amazed at how many times they found themselves resisting new suggestions because they triggered painful memories from the past. Peter found that every time the discussion turned to job searching, he would start thinking about the ex-boss who had made his life miserable. In letting this happen, he was allowing an unpleasant experience from the past to overshadow his plans for the future. If he wasn't good enough last time, how could he succeed this time?

I suggested to Peter that he try saying the word 'stop' inwardly every time the thought arose. This is a popular and easy way to improve your concentration by keeping unwanted thoughts at bay. It worked perfectly for Peter, and for several other clients, who have made it a regular part of their daily routine.

Christine found it easier to relate to a visual image. For weeks, she had been lying awake at night worrying over a personal problem. She was relieved to discover that she could banish her worries by imagining herself writing them down on a piece of paper, then setting fire to it. Dumping her troubles into an imaginary bin was another exercise that produced measurable results.

Rob found it difficult to use inner talk or mental images, but related well to more tangible prompts. He devised his own 'happy hints' by drawing smiling faces on adhesive notes and sticking them around the house and office. Fortunately, being the gregarious type, he didn't mind when his colleagues and family teased him about his artistic efforts.

Personal affirmations are yet another way to overcome defeatist attitudes, particularly if you are prone to self-criticism. They allow us to take the idea of intercepting negative thoughts a step further by using positive self-talk to tell ourselves that what we want has already come true.

Let's say you have got into the habit of delivering energy-sapping messages to yourself, such as: 'I haven't got the nerve to ask for a pay rise' or 'It's too late for me to change.' The more you entertain these thoughts, the more likely they are to come true. Intercepting the negative messages, and switching them off, will certainly help, but replacing them with a positive statement is even more powerful.

The statement you use should be brief, positive and in the present tense. In the first instance you could try saying: 'I am strong, confident and ready to ask for a pay rise.' In the second: 'Every day I feel stronger and stronger about accepting change.' Writing your affirmations down will act as a memory jogger, and using coloured pens or graphics will add a powerful visual stimulus to the process. They work best when repeated on a regular basis, and certainly have more chance of taking hold when used immediately after practising deep relaxation.

Finally, a technique that may help if you find yourself forced to work with someone you dislike, and there is no way out of the relationship in the short term. Try focusing on the other person's good points. Everyone has something we can admire, if we only take the trouble to look for it. Doing this will, at the very least, buy you time while you look for a better solution. At its best, it can have a subtle effect on the other party, and help them react more favourably to you.

Simple though they are, these refocusing methods illustrate that we usually have a choice about the thoughts we entertain. When we go with the negative drift, our energy is diminished, and we grow ever more judgmental and petty. When we systematically turn our attention to the positive, the opposite happens; not only do we feel better about ourselves and those around us, but we become more attractive to other people. Experiment with the above until you find something that suits you.

Listing Achievements

In job search training sessions, people are often asked to list their achievements. This can bring some surprising results.

Despite running a successful retail business for over ten years, all Don could focus on was the shame of closing down when the rent for his shop became unreasonably high. It took weeks to help him see that setting up from scratch and providing years of employment for two assistants were highly marketable achievements. 'Anyone could do it,' he insisted. Eventually he realized that this was patently untrue. It took flair, business acumen and dedication; certainly not things that *anyone* could do.

Varsha had no such reservations about her accomplishments. She had worked only intermittently during the past twenty years, but this did not prevent her producing a respectable list of achievements, largely centring on running the home and helping two of her children to get to university. She also had the knack of describing what she had done in terms of organizational and motivational skills that could be readily transferred to the workplace.

These contrasting examples show that appreciating our achievements is largely a matter of confidence. Making the effort to identify them is a powerful way to boost your self-esteem. It is not a question of being boastful, but of being able to take justifiable pride in your accomplishments. This is a habit worth cultivating, because when it comes to impressing employers, you will need to have a store of successes at your fingertips, and be ready to explain them without hesitation.

Exercise

Clocking up your successes is an excellent way to feel good about yourself, which in turn makes you feel better about other people. Try listing a few personal achievements now. There may be some obvious examples from your work, such as introducing new ideas or saving money, but think too about other areas of your life, past and present. Have you been successful in organizing college or community events, captained a sports team or won a significant award at school? For the time being, forget about what employers will make of them; that will be covered later. Right now we are concerned only with your self-esteem.

Achievements

How did you find the exercise? Was it easy, or did you find yourself struggling? Whatever your experience, making an effort to understand your own worth plays an important part in staying on a positive track. Keep your list up-to-date, and make sure you refer to it on a regular basis. In Part Two, we will examine how this will also save time when it comes to making career choices, compiling your CV and preparing for interviews.

Learning from the Entrepreneurs

There are certain individuals who have a remarkable talent for leading successful enterprises, and turning around seemingly impossible situations. These people have a lot to teach us in terms of attitude.

In the past, 'entrepreneur' was a term reserved for captains of industry and other successful business people. But times have changed. In the future, we will all have to become more entrepreneurial, not just in terms of how we do our jobs, but in how we market our skills to a wider variety of employers and service users. In the millennium, consumers will become more and more demanding and 'customer service' will be important in all jobs. 'Customers' can be anyone, from the people who buy your organization's goods or services, to your fellow workers. They all have one thing in common; the desire to feel good about whatever it is they are buying. In modern times, everyone is looking for the feelgood factor, and the individual who delivers this will reap the rewards financially and emotionally.

If you think about your own motivation in buying one product rather than another, you will see that the difference often lies in how it makes you *feel*. For instance, if the mobile phone had been marketed as a piece of emergency equipment, rather than a lifestyle item, it is unlikely to have become the 'must have' status symbol it is today. Marketeers and advertisers are experts in making people feel good, and the successful entrepreneurs are those who make the consumer want their product, and theirs alone, no matter how good competing brands may be.

Education may not be the first area to spring to mind when entrepreneurial skills are under discussion, but it in recent years head teachers have had to learn to combine their training responsibilities with talents more commonly associated with corporate executives. William Atkinson, head teacher at the Phoenix High School in West London, is a vibrant example of this phenomenon in action. I first met William when I worked with him on a project at another school. I was very impressed by the enthusiasm he managed to generate all around him, and it came as no surprise when I heard that he had been head-hunted to rescue a poorly performing school on the verge of closure.

When William took over at the new school in 1995, it was notorious for poor exam results, and attracting too few pupils to justify being kept open. Overall, the problem was considered to be 'unfixable' and William was brought in as a last-ditch attempt to turn things around.

One of the first things he did was to get together with his team and come up with a new name for the school. 'Phoenix', the mythical bird that rose from the ashes, was an inspired choice, creating a potent image of renewal and hope. The team followed this through by designing a smart new uniform that pupils were obviously proud to wear. William also made a point of being highly visible around the school, regularly touring the premises to keep up-to-date with the pupils' aspirations and concerns.

This positive approach produced outstanding results in a comparatively short time. By the end of 1997, pupils achieving grade A–C in their exam results had increased by 300 per cent and the number joining had risen from 46 to 174. Of these, 140 made the school their first choice.

Although William has stayed on at the school, he is now also in great demand as an adviser to the government and various high-profile industrial committees, which involves him in regular television appearances. Everyone wants to know how he transformed such a seemingly hopeless establishment by boosting morale and performance to the point where parents are clamouring to find places for their children.

Restoring the school's fortunes in this way obviously took a tremendous amount of hard work on the part of teaching staff and pupils. But this alone was not enough. The deciding factor was William's absolute belief that the job could be done; in short, his positive attitude won the day.

William's own assessment of the transformation is that it is a classic example of good teamwork, and he gives his staff a great deal of the credit for what was achieved. This is typical of strong leaders, who keep morale high by scrupulously giving credit where it is due. On a personal level, he attributes much of his success to consistently stepping out of his comfort zone, and following up each project with something that stretches him even further.

So what are the learning points for your own career development?

- Know exactly what you want to achieve and hold on to the vision.
- When faced with challenges, cultivate an attitude of 'can do', rather than surrendering to defeatist feelings.
- Be constantly on the alert for new, improved ways of doing things.
- Practise extending your comfort zone by taking on new ventures, no matter how small.
- Listen to what other people have to say; their input is vital to your success.
- Always give credit to others when they contribute to your achievements.
- 'Packaging' is important; pay attention to your image.

You don't need qualifications to think like an entrepreneur, nor does it matter what your current profession or aspirations are. You can start anywhere. When a junior clerk asked me what she could do to get started, I suggested that she overhaul the office filing system. This may sound simplistic, but the activity itself is beside the point. The objective is to train yourself to see things more creatively and learn to leave your personal stamp on everything you do. Regard everyone you come into contact with at work as your 'customer' and set about giving them the best possible service. This is the way to develop a reputation for quality at all levels, and establish a unique selling-point for yourself.

Encouraging Feedback

Most of us react favourably to praise, but getting feedback on our weak points can sometimes be very uncomfortable. As a protective measure, we may try to justify our performance or behaviour, rather than facing up to making changes. This is a great pity because it means we often miss out on one of the very best ways to make progress in our careers. If we don't listen carefully to what other people have to say about us, there is a good chance of a mismatch between how we think we are coming across and how we are actually perceived. It may therefore come as a nasty shock when the truth finally catches up with us.

This is yet another area where a simple shift of focus can come to your rescue. Next time you find yourself bristling when someone makes a negative comment about you, think about how the top performing companies encourage their customers to give them feedback. They expend huge amounts of time and energy analysing complaints and customer surveys to see where they can make improvements in their products or services. This represents a sound investment on their part, allowing them to tailor their offerings ever more closely to the consumer's needs. You should aim to do the same with your skills.

When feedback comes your way, remind yourself to take an entrepreneurial view. Business leaders have no time to take offence when they are criticized by customers or advisers. To them the only failure is a failure to learn from the things that go wrong. Once you are able to think of your skills and abilities as a 'product', it should be easier to react positively to comments on your performance.

You should also keep in mind that when comments are unduly negative or personal, it is often because the person responsible is not skilled in giving constructive feedback. Their opinions may be perfectly valid, but they simply lack the ability to get them across in a diplomatic way. If you find yourself a victim of this type of ineptitude, use assertiveness techniques to depersonalize the situation, and comfort yourself with the fact that you are getting *free* input on how to make your 'product' more competitive. Marketeers would jump at the chance to get such valuable information without having to pay a penny for it.

If you are working, you may be lucky enough to have regular

appraisals, so make the most of these by actively listening to what is being said and following through with an action plan to address areas where there is a need for improvement. If your manager doesn't come up with any ideas, take the initiative yourself. For instance, look for an opportunity to negotiate some training that will stand you in good stead for the future.

Be aware, too, of the growing popularity of the 360 degree appraisal, where employees are judged not only by the boss, but by a range of other people, who may include peers, customers, suppliers, and even family members. Although well intentioned, this can be a daunting prospect for any of us, and completely terrifying for people who are over-sensitive to criticism. When faced with a 360 degree appraisal, it is essential to understand that people are being asked to assess your performance in certain areas of your job, not to make judgments about you as a person. With a range of people involved, you are also likely to get a far more balanced picture than when you have to rely on the opinion of just one person.

If you are self-employed, or thinking about taking the plunge in the future, it will be vital to put your performance under rigid scrutiny on a regular basis. As well as getting guidance from business advisers, stay in touch with what your customers want by asking for their opinion of what you have to offer and how you perform. Self-discipline is paramount; nothing can be left to chance when commercial interests are at stake.

And of course you should never miss out on the prospect of *free* feedback from a job interview, something we will discuss in Chapter Eleven.

Giving Constructive Criticism

So far we have concentrated on how to receive feedback, but it is every bit as important to be diplomatic when you are the one responsible for the assessment or criticism.

Brian left his job to get away from a boss he described as a whinger: 'He was always criticizing me in front of other people but as soon as I decided to leave, he couldn't praise me enough.

But it was too little, too late. I can get a job anywhere; I don't have to put up with being humiliated.'

Brian's boss is not alone in lacking the ability to deliver feedback without hurting and demoralizing others. We are all guilty of this at times, whether or not we are in a management position. In general, the more assertive we are, the less likely we are to cause offence in everyday situations. However, there are a few further rules to be observed when you have to give a formal appraisal or deliver a reprimand:

⟹ Always preserve confidentiality by holding the meeting in private.
⟹ Don't jump in with your views; start by getting the other person's perspective.
⟹ Stick to the facts and avoid speculation about their motivation.
⟹ Give a balanced view by starting with the person's strengths.
⟹ Don't impose an action plan, but try to come to a mutually agreeable solution.

If Brian's boss had stuck to these guidelines, he would have preserved goodwill and saved himself the expense of recruiting and training a new employee.

SUMMARY

* Maintaining a positive attitude pays dividends at work and when job hunting.
* There are a variety of techniques to help you guard against negative tendencies.
* Keeping a journal of personal successes will boost your self-esteem and provide up-to-date input for your CV.
* Learn from the entrepreneurs and cultivate an attitude of 'can do' at work.
* Be open to feedback; the only failure is failure to learn from the things that go wrong.

Chapter Seven

The Art of Networking

Personal recommendations play
a huge part in spreading the word
about your capabilities. The wider
your sphere of influence, the
better your chances of gaining
promotion or being offered a new
job or assignment.

Expanding Your Grapevine

Networking is about establishing and nourishing relationships
that further your career or business interests. It is tremendously
rewarding, and one of the best ways to create your own luck in
the new world of work, where opportunities abound if you only
know where to look.

In the preceding chapters you have learned how to create inner
harmony and develop strong organizational and interpersonal
skills. Now comes the time to put these talents to use in widening
your circle of contacts and supporters. This combination of inner
strength and outward support is the ultimate secret of survival in
times of uncertainty and constant change. Despite this, many
people make little attempt to network until they are actively
looking for a job, which is a mistake. Certainly, it is an important
part of job searching, but from now on we will all have to stay
constantly on the alert for new opportunities, which means that
networking must be an ongoing part of our lives.

If you have any doubts about this, let me give you ten specific
reasons why. Networking can help you to:

- make career choices
- find a new job or assignment
- advertise your abilities and services
- get promoted
- enter into partnerships and joint ventures
- secure references
- keep your knowledge and skills up-to-date
- make yourself interesting
- keep your morale high
- attract the head-hunters

Choosing a career is a matter of matching your aspirations and abilities to one or more professions. Advisers and books provide invaluable guidance, but talking to the people who are already operating in the field will complete the picture for you. This is an ideal way to look behind the scenes and get an understanding of the reality that lies beneath the job description.

Job leads are generated from a variety of sources, but if you limit yourself to advertised vacancies you will miss out on the hidden market of opportunities that are never advertised. This is even more true for people working on a self-employed basis, whose survival is often dependent on the tips they pick up from personal and professional contacts.

Personal recommendations also play a huge part in spreading the word about your capabilities. The wider your sphere of influence, the better your chances of gaining promotion or being offered new assignments. People feel much safer about offering responsibility to someone they consider to be tried and tested. The same goes for self-employed professionals, who are often looking to expand their interests by going into partnership with someone else.

Getting references can be a problem when previous employers go out of business or restructure, something that has proved a barrier for several of my clients. When this happens, a recommendation from someone on your list of contacts can often provide an acceptable alternative. Likewise, if you have worked for a large corporation, you may find they only provide a bland standardized reference, so it can help to balance this with a glowing testimonial from someone on your grapevine.

Business gatherings are fertile ground for picking up ideas, and an informal word here or there can be worth weeks of poring over journals or surfing the Internet for information. They also allow you to:

➡ learn from state-of-the art presentations
➡ watch how the top people put themselves across
➡ stay on top of the latest trends in training and qualifications

Staying in circulation is even more essential when you are unemployed or between assignments. As well as being useful in finding work, it keeps your morale high and gives you an interest. This in turn makes you more interesting to other people, and you will be less likely to pick up a 'victim' tag.

Attracting the attention of head-hunters, also known as executive search consultants, is the holy grail of ambitious professionals everywhere. Naturally, you are free to contact them yourself, but if you have established a reputation for excellence it makes it far easier for them to find you. Pro-active networking is one way to keep your profile high enough to work your way on to their 'hit-list', although it would be unfair to suggest that there is a fail-safe way to do this. In reality, you are far more likely to be head-hunted by another department within your existing organization or be approached directly by a competitor.

Sarah, a customer service manager, discovered the truth of this when she was sought out by a company based in the same office block as her employer. Against a backdrop of redundancies and low morale, Sarah maintained her professionalism and continued to interact cheerfully with everyone she met, including staff from the other companies in the building. When the time came for one of these organizations to recruit new staff, discreet enquiries about her abilities produced nothing but the highest praise from the people around her. Without lifting a finger, she found herself invited to an interview, which resulted in an exciting new job in an expanding company. Her secret was a genuine interest in other people, combined with a total commitment to quality in all areas of her activity.

Getting Started

People

You can network with people from any area of your life, whether or not they are involved in your work or business activities. Ideas and tips can come from any source, and they may pave the way to more specific leads in the future. The information itself is less important than how energetic you are in using it. Liam, one of my job search clients, was so inspired during a networking training session that he phoned his brother-in-law the same evening. His brother-in-law was unable to help directly, but gave him another contact. This led to five more calls, landing Liam a job within weeks.

No doubt you already have a significant number of contacts, although you may never have thought of them as being able to further your career aims. Everyone has to start somewhere: it is much easier to begin with people you already know, then, as your confidence grows, expand your horizons by actively seeking to add to your list.

Use the following checklist to get an idea of how large your existing network may be:

Family ☐
Friends ☐
Fellow students ☐
Teachers or lecturers ☐
Business associates ☐
Colleagues/Managers ☐
Advisers ☐
Suppliers ☐
Customers/Clients ☐
Religious leaders ☐

Counsellors/Therapists ☐
Hairdressers ☐
Doctors/Dentists ☐

Additions

Places

There are no rules about where to network; you may decide to start by casually chatting to friends and family. However, if you are serious about climbing the ladder, the wider you cast your net, the greater your chances of success. What you choose will depend on your lifestyle and ambitions, but aim for a mix of business and social venues.

Here are some ideas that may help you.

Professional and Trade Associations/Institutes

There are a wide range of organizations that you may be eligible to join, depending on your profession or the industry or sector in which you work. Others, such as Chambers of Commerce, draw members from all commercial areas.

Although some associations may appear to confine membership to managers or directors, you may well find they are more flexible in practice. These days, hierarchical structures are less important, as companies trim the fat by cutting out whole layers of management and devolve responsibility further and further down the line. Likewise, as more people turn to self-employment and contract work, they are effectively becoming 'directors' of their own one-person operations. Bear this in mind when you are looking for a suitable establishment. If in doubt, just pick up the phone and ask. If you have no idea about what to join, try the Yellow Pages or check out the business directories and trade journals at your local library.

Be careful to investigate the establishment thoroughly before parting with any subscription fees or other payments. Any worthwhile organization should allow you to make a reconnaissance trip before you make a firm commitment. Alternatively, you may be able to go along as someone else's guest, which will give you hands-on experience of how they operate. You can take this idea further by joining up with friends and associates to try out a number of establishments. If each person joins something different, they can invite the others as guests and share useful information.

Use the following to help you evaluate what's on offer. Do they have:

➤ specific networking events, such as breakfasts, lunches, weekend gatherings ☐
➤ opportunities to update your knowledge and skills via regular meetings, training events, conferences or workshops ☐
➤ newsletters via mail or the Internet ☐
➤ if you are self-employed, journals where you can advertise your services ☐

Voluntary and Charitable Work

Even if you are already in paid work, involvement with voluntary or charitable organizations can be an excellent way to broaden your experience, as well as bringing you the satisfaction of doing something worthwhile. I have known many people who have added to their skills in this way, and made some valuable contacts in the process. It also fills embarrassing gaps on a CV and can be just as impressive as paid work when it comes to an interview.

Clubs and Gyms

Despite their informal setting, a lot of business is done at clubs and leisure centres. In these situations, people are at their most relaxed, and may be less cautious about parting with useful tips than they would be at a business gathering.

Company Events

Never underestimate the importance of social gatherings and 'fun' events organized by your company. Social skills are just as interesting to management as your performance at work. Getting involved in the organization of these get-togethers can certainly take you up a notch or two in their estimation. For instance, you may only be working in the mail room, with little opportunity to shine, but helping with the arrangements for a large-scale event may give you a unique opportunity to show off hidden talents.

College and University Associations

If you are a graduate, keep in touch with other ex-students by joining an alumni network. Make an effort to sustain friendships that have sprouted on campus by attending social gatherings and keeping in regular telephone contact. You may also secure introductions to people from earlier generations, who are now established in influential positions.

Outplacement Centres and Government Training Schemes

Privately run outplacement centres and government training schemes and job clubs provide the perfect opportunity for job-seekers to team up socially and professionally. In some cases they act as a lifeline that prevents depression setting in. Quite apart from the training, there is the advantage of having a group of people with a common aim, all looking out for each other. Friendships formed in this way can last a lifetime, as can the networking opportunities they provide.

Other Suggestions

⮕ community groups
⮕ over 40s clubs
⮕ evening classes
⮕ hotels and bars
⮕ parent teacher associations
⮕ women's organizations
⮕ disability groups
⮕ sports events

As you can see, there is no end to the places where you can network. Use this opportunity to make a note of anything you are already involved in, then start to think about whether you need to expand your interests.

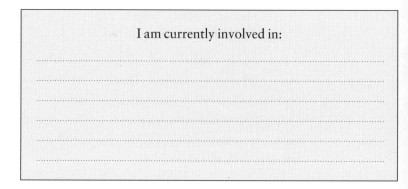

I am currently involved in:

The Process

At social gatherings you can afford to be casual and spontaneous in your approach. Some friendly questions and a hint here and there should be enough to find out whether someone is in a position to help you. The last thing you want is to scare off your friends and acquaintances by being too forthright or pushy.

However, the business variety needs to be tackled in a far more structured way. Although it is customary to appear laid back and relaxed, this is often the result of hard work and years of practice. The veterans may be able to play it by ear, but beginners need to keep in mind that there are three essential stages in the process:

➧ preparation
➧ interaction
➧ follow-up

Preparation

If you are going to a business gathering of any kind, or engaging in a leisure pursuit where you are likely to meet other professionals, make sure you have a set of business cards with you. Don't worry if your company doesn't provide cards, or you can't afford to have them printed professionally. The type produced by the machines you find in shopping malls and stations are perfectly acceptable. They should also give you a choice of styles and layouts. Alternatively, if you have a personal computer, try designing your own.

The details on your card will vary according to your situation. For instance, someone with professional qualifications, who is well established in a company, might have a card that looks like this:

ABC Company
_____

Address, xxxxxxxxxxx, xxxxxxxx, xxxxxxxxxxxx, xxxxxxxx

Chris Jones MBA
Director

Telephone +44 (0)0000 000000
Fax +44 (0)0000 000000
E-mail cjones@abccompany.etc

However, networking is not the preserve of executives and people well established in their careers. Many of the individuals who attend gatherings are just starting out, or between jobs, and may not have a qualification to their name. Looking through the cards I have collected at various functions, I counted several that show only a name, address and telephone number. Between these and the fully-fledged corporate card, I found a variety of permutations. The moral is not to get hung up about your card; there are no rules about content or layout.

Self-employed consultants and company representatives may also have flyers or brochures, which go into more detail about their services. Whether or not they use them depends on the nature of the gathering.

By contrast, a diary or personal organizer is essential. To those of you with a hectic schedule, this will be obvious, but there is an equally compelling reason for the others among you. You must, at all times, give the impression of having lots to do. Never mind if your diary is clear for the next ten years; nobody need know this but you. Busy people are deemed to be successful and interesting, so don't commit the cardinal sin of saying, 'I haven't got anything lined up, so I can come over any time.' Whatever the truth of the matter, if someone suggests a meeting, always take out your diary or personal organizer, and spend a little time looking through it before you commit yourself.

Checking out the dress code is also important. You don't want to turn up in a sharp suit if the emphasis is smart-casual. If you have done your homework and made a reconnaissance trip, this should be easy enough.

Prepare yourself for questions by doing an audit of your skills and abilities, but be ready to converse on a wider range of topics. Keep yourself interesting by reading up on current affairs and what's going on in the business arena.

Interaction

Carla runs a busy management consultancy, and is by any standards a highly successful and confident woman. At networking gatherings, she draws people like a magnet, and always comes armed with a reserve of witty comments and anecdotes. Imagine then how surprised I was to hear how reluctant she is to go along at all: 'I really have to steel myself to attend these things; talking to all those people can be such a strain.'

Take heart from this if you are at all worried about how you will come across. Lots of people share your anxieties, but they have learned to overcome them. This is where deep-breathing techniques can work wonders, and make you feel better straight away. If you can't think of anything to say, ask people questions about themselves and their work. You may be amazed at the positive response this produces. However, don't probe too deeply or get too serious. A sense of humour is a great asset, but trying to loosen up with alcohol is a mistake. Keep your head clear by drinking in moderation or, better still, stick to mineral water or fruit juice.

You will inevitably have to brace yourself to approach people you don't know. Sometimes you will be warmly received, on other occasions you may be cold-shouldered. Don't worry about it; this is a percentages game. Regard your early efforts as a rehearsal; as time goes by, your performance will get better and better. Don't be overwhelmed if you find yourself moving amongst senior and influential people. If you hold your nerve, they will accept you on equal terms and recommend you to others accordingly. People at the top of their profession are usually socially at ease, and many of them take great pleasure in helping others along the way.

Whatever you do, don't bear down on fellow participants brandishing flyers and brochures. The same goes for your CV. Even if you are attending a promotional event or a specific networking get-together, take your cue from the veterans. If you find that other people get straight down to business, by all means follow their example. If in doubt, play it safe; overtly predatory behaviour will only mark you out as an amateur. Keep your cool, and wait until the time is right before whipping out your card or brochure. Nor is it a good idea to produce your CV the moment someone asks about your work, which may show you in a desperate light. You can always offer to send it on later.

If you identify an interesting prospect, exchange cards, and ask if it will be all right to phone them at a mutually convenient time in the future. That way they will be more likely to remember who you are when the call comes through.

It is also vital to remember that networking is a two-way affair. There is nothing wrong with prospecting for contacts, but you should pay equal attention to how you can help the people you meet. This is how to keep things in perspective and make the whole process more rewarding. It will also take the tension out of new and challenging situations, where self-absorption can lead to conversational paralysis.

Don't expect too much, too quickly. Although my very first excursion to a Chamber of Commerce event resulted in a highly profitable assignment, it can often take months, even years, to get results of this magnitude. In the short term, you are more likely to pick up ideas and information which will require dedicated follow-up. That said, it can be breathtaking when a contact you haven't seen for some time suddenly calls to offer you a job or the chance to run a project.

Follow-up

Over time you are likely to end up with a collection of business cards and a list of 'prospects'. To make the most of this, set up a specific logging system to keep track of the people you have met and the information they have given you. This log will also form part of the career portfolio discussed in the next chapter.

Let's assume you have met someone who works for an expanding organization that is likely to be creating some interesting job opportunities in the future. They have told you it is too early to make an approach, but they will phone you as soon as there are any developments. What do you do now? Wait around and hope they will come through for you? Most definitely not; once you have created an opening, nothing should be left to chance. This clearly calls for an entry in your records, which might look as follows:

Name:	Hope Fulle
Company:	XYZ Consultancy
Telephone:	* * * *
Fax:	* * * *
E-mail:	* * * *
Where met:	X Healthclub
Date:	* * * *
Position:	senior business analyst – 5 years with company.
Comments:	XYZ Company expanding; new jobs being created. Promised to phone when more news is available.
Action:	Make follow-up phone call in 8 weeks. In meantime, find out more about company.

In the above case, you would also make a simultaneous diary entry for the due date, such as: 'Phone Hope Fulle – see contact file (journal, card or whatever system used).' As you got to know the person better, you would expand the comments section to make sure your information was always completely up-to-date.

Keeping precise records like this allows you to build up a profile of the people you meet, and makes follow-up far easier. However, never pass on personal details or confidential information to a third party. And never pass on anything at all to someone who may capitalize on it before you do. When you are in the business of self-marketing, it is vital to maintain your competitive edge by keeping your trade secrets close to your chest at all times.

It also pays to remember that little things mean a lot when it comes to building relationships, so take care to thank people when they help you. Keep a supply of 'Thank You' cards or notelets, and always handwrite the message. A personalized greeting creates a far better impression than a hastily despatched e-mail or fax.

The Internet

The Internet is a very effective way to interact with people, even if your meetings remain confined to cyberspace. I once ran a project at IBM, where local students used the company's network as part of their French language studies. Via the network, I enlisted the help of staff in Paris, Montreal, Geneva and Brussels, who 'conversed' in French with the students via e-mail. Despite the fact that neither I nor the students ever met our correspondents in person, the exchange had a profound effect on all of us. It enlivened the whole process of learning another language, and we all felt a strong bond with our overseas helpers.

That was over twelve years ago, when linking up in cyberspace was not the everyday activity it is now. Since then, global e-mail communications and websites have become common features of business and domestic life. More and more jobs are being advertised on the Internet, and many companies and agencies use on-line CV formats and application forms. Colleges and universities are following their lead, and some even offer employers and former students recruitment services across the net. These are developments that cannot be ignored. The message is clear: if you want to get ahead, it pays to get connected.

If you don't have a PC, or cannot afford a web connection at the moment, think about using the services of a cybercafé. As well as learning to surf the net and use e-mail, you may also identify some useful contacts amongst your fellow customers. Don't despair if the very idea of the Internet strikes terror into your heart. I have met many people who felt like this, usually because they had never tried it. The good news is that they usually lose their fear as soon as they are shown how easy it is to pick up the basics. The worst part is worrying about the unknown, so if you are letting this get in your way, book some training now. If a friend or someone in the family is willing to help, so much the better.

Making it Happen

Networking will undoubtedly open doors for you, but only if you have the courage to knock. There is never a right time to start, and most people feel a little apprehensive about it at first. There is actually nothing to fear; all it takes is a little research and regular practice. If money is a problem, start by exploring opportunities in your current sphere of activity, then build up as your finances improve. Expanding your circle of contacts is not a luxury, but something that should be at the very heart of your career management/job-search campaign.

SUMMARY

* Networking is about establishing relationships that further your career and boost your chances of finding the right job.
* The wider your circle of contacts, the easier it will be to find work, get promoted and maintain a high profile.
* You can network with people from any area of your life, at social and business events.
* To be effective, it must be an ongoing process, not something you leave until you are out of work.
* Building a database of contacts and getting to grips with the Internet adds to your chances of success.

Part Two

The Millennium Campaign Plan

Chapter Eight

Managing Your Own Career

Successfully managing your own career demands optimum use of organizational and interpersonal skills, plus a firm commitment to lifelong learning.

Developing Career Resilience

In Part One you learned how to embrace the challenge of change with renewed confidence. Now comes the time to put your creative energy to work on a career management plan that will sustain you for the rest of your working life. Knowing how to make informed choices and take responsibility for your own development is vital for your future prosperity.

The starting point is to appreciate why you must develop *career resilience*, and how this differs from the traditional approach to career planning. The latter entails choosing an occupation or sector, then working your way up the ladder in your chosen profession or business area. Although this remains a valid option, there is no longer any certainty that it will mean job security in the future. Redundancy and other misfortunes can strike at any time, with disastrous consequences for those who have not planned ahead.

By contrast, developing career resilience means anticipating that you will work for a variety of employers or clients during your working life, and ensuring that you broaden your experience and skills base as you go. In this way, you build up a 'portfolio' of expertise, which can be used in a range of roles and sectors, possibly in a mix of part-time, contract or self-employed work. You may well start in the traditional way, but you must accept that your employer is unlikely to need you indefinitely, and make sure you stay on top of developments in the job market. It is this pioneering spirit that makes the difference between staying in demand and becoming a victim of circumstances.

Paul did not have career resilience in mind when he joined a consultancy firm as an assistant business analyst, but he did relish the prospect of working on a variety of projects for diverse organizations. Although he is employed on a full-time, permanent basis, and plans to stay with the company for the foreseeable future, this diversity of experience would make him very attractive to other organizations should he become available in the future. He would also be well placed to set up on a self-employed basis, with a high earnings potential. In short, he has made an excellent career choice.

Kerrie is a young hairdresser, with a clear vision of where she wants her career to go. She is currently building up her skills base by training as an aromatherapist, which will give her another outlet for her creative abilities and people skills. Kerrie will not leave hairdressing, but intends to reduce her hours as she builds up a base of aromatherapy clients. Her longer-term plans include training in other therapies and joining up with like-minded professionals to open a health and beauty clinic. Her main focus is not on becoming wealthy, but on earning her living by doing the things for which she has a real passion.

Although both of the above examples involve young people, it is just as important to stay flexible in later life. When people have years of experience behind them, redundancy is often the catalyst to explore new opportunities. The choices they make are as different as the individuals involved, although self-employment is an increasingly popular option, with consultancy work being high on the list.

If it is so easy to re-invent oneself, why, then, do so many people find themselves trapped in a series of low paid, dead-end jobs? The answer is that it is not easy, but the result of hard work. Successfully managing your own career demands optimum use of organizational and interpersonal skills, plus a firm commitment to lifelong learning. It means taking the helm and steering your own course. Naturally, you will need help along the way, but the difference between success and failure is largely in your own hands.

Looked at in this way, no job need be regarded as hopeless. Everything you do adds to your portfolio of skills and increases your value accordingly. Once again, the secret is not what you do, but how you approach life and what you learn from your experiences.

Your Personal Portfolio

From now on, you will need to make a concerted effort to document your marketable expertise and log anything that influences your career development. Recognize that you are in the business of selling your abilities, and get working on your sales material right now.

Whatever your situation or age, you undoubtedly already have something that will be of value to prospective employers or clients. Despite this, you would be surprised at the number of people, at all levels, who make very little attempt to chart their progress as they go along. It can be painful to watch as individuals struggle to recall their achievements, or to hear how they repeatedly undersell themselves in interviews. Failure to plan ahead can be a costly mistake.

One way to avoid this pitfall is to open your own portfolio. Effective career management requires the highest degree of organization, and all your materials must be readily accessible. Use any system that appeals to you, but make sure it is durable and easily expanded. Remember, it will be with you for the rest of your working life, and is likely to grow at an impressive rate. A computerized system is fine, but you will need an accompanying manual file for formal documentation, such as educational certificates.

The contents of your file will include:

- an ongoing record of your skills, achievements, qualifications and learning
- details of your networking contacts, prospective employers, advisers, agencies and any other organizations or individuals having a bearing on your career
- the results of your research activities (covered later in this chapter)
- your CVs (you will probably have several versions – see next chapter)
- sample covering letters to employers
- notes and feedback from interviews and other meetings

Apart from its obvious organizational advantages, compiling a portfolio will work wonders for your confidence. The effect can be magical, as previously unacknowledged talents begin to emerge in a such a powerfully tangible form. Capitalise on this by making your file as attractive as possible, with maximum use of colour and graphics.

Get started by organizing any material you already have. As you progress, make sure you file everything else of relevance, making notes and taking photocopies as necessary.

Making Choices

Whether or not you are faced with an immediate career choice, this is a good time to get acquainted with the mechanics of decision-making. At the very least, you should make an effort to identify the things you are good at, and keep yourself up-to-date with job opportunities. Changes can happen with frightening speed, and you never know when you will be faced with a sudden transition.

The ways and means of arriving at clearcut career goals are many and varied, and there is no room here to explore all the angles. However, the following should give you sufficient insight into the process to enable you to use your own imagination and follow up with well-directed research.

Life Goals and Personal Values

As we saw in Chapter Four, no matter where you are starting from, whether you have a great deal of experience behind you or are just leaving college or school, planning your career begins with understanding how you want your life to look in the future. Your work can never be counted a success if it makes you unhappy or takes you away from the people and things you love.

If you have not already done the 'life goals' exercise, set aside some time to do it in the near future, and file the result in the front of your portfolio. This will help you to stay on course whenever your resolution starts to waver. Conversely, you may have to revisit your plans if career considerations become a larger part of the equation.

Your personal values should also be taken into account when you make your career choices. For example, do you want to make a lot of money or are you more concerned about having a pleasant working environment? Are company ethics more important to you than promotion prospects? Would you be willing to trade a steady income for the chance to take your own risks and work independently?

Interests

Your general interests may also point you in the direction of an occupational area or specific profession, as we shall see later. For now, just make a note of them:

Achievements and Skills

The next step is to define what you have to *offer* to prospective employers or clients. Once you understand this, you can begin the task of matching your capabilities and aspirations to the requirements of specific professions and organizations.

As we saw in Chapter Six, people sometimes find it difficult to give themselves full credit for their accomplishments. For instance, did you manage to produce a list of achievements? If not, this is another essential task for your 'to do' list. Achievements can highlight hidden talents and reveal the activities that give us real pleasure. Any or all of these may be directly transferable into a new or first career. The results of leisure interests should never be ignored; this is how a bank manager can become a sports therapist or a sales assistant set up a catering business.

Go through the list again, then prioritize items in order of their significance to you personally. Next, think about the skills you used to get the desired results, and write them down for future reference. Add any other practical abilities or areas of specialization that you have acquired through your experience at work or elsewhere. Think too about how you can be of use to *others*. Cultivating a genuine interest in how you can be of service to other people, whether they are employers or customers, puts your own needs and wants into perspective and prevents you from becoming too self-centred.

If you are still struggling, the following should give you a broad idea of what to look for. It is not intended as a comprehensive guide, so make sure you add your own ideas.

administrating	being creative
persuading	managing
analysing	computing
generating ideas	serving
counselling	working with figures
recording	selling
making things	caring for customers
designing	planning
organizing	communicating in writing or verbally
repairing	training

Don't be tempted to rush this exercise. The key to career flexibility lies in having an in-depth understanding of your skills base. This is your 'product', and before you start to identify potential buyers, you must have a strong belief in the value of what you have to sell.

Things, Data and People

Another way to determine your strengths and preferences is to categorise your key skills into working with *things*, *data* or *people*. Obviously there will be a degree of overlap, but look for the predominant factor.

Things   This involves working with tools, machinery, electrical equipment and vehicles. It includes building, construction, motoring and engineering. On the creative side, it might involve making things by hand, such as pottery and other arts and crafts.

Data   Working with data means processing and analysing facts and figures or disseminating information. It almost certainly involves using computers and other electronic equipment, and lends itself well to working remotely from your employer or clients as a teleworker.

People   Although all work involves some contact with people, here the main focus is on helping, directing or persuading others. Occupations range from counselling and nursing to teaching and tourism.

Characteristics

Your personal characteristics also play a part in the type of work and roles that suit you. For instance, if you have identified leadership qualities from work or other pursuits, it might be worth considering management opportunities. Someone who is outgoing and persuasive might be attracted to sales or any number of positions that involve working with, or influencing, people.

To get a balanced picture, you also need to understand your

limitations. These may be no more than temporary barriers, which can be overcome by self-discipline or training. On the other hand, they may be a fundamental part of your character, which it would not be appropriate to change.

Training and Qualifications

Your existing training and qualifications may be of a general nature or career-specific. In either case, they will certainly have a sales value, but take care that they don't limit your outlook. Just because you have been trained in one particular area does not mean that you have to stay within those limits if your circumstances change. There may be many other possibilities if you are prepared to keep an open mind, and consider retraining where necessary. So many people never discover their full potential because they are afraid to stretch themselves, preferring to settle for what they think will be a safe option.

Visualization Exercise

By now you should have some idea of where your real interests lie and what you have to offer, even if this is not yet pointing you at any particular role.

There is still some way to go, but take this opportunity to focus your attention, by summarizing what you have uncovered so far.

Life goals:

Values:

Interests:

Key achievements:

Main skills and abilities:

Preference – things, data or people:

Characteristics:

Training and qualifications:

Now that you have a snapshot of your 'product', it's time to put your imagination to work and indulge in a little fantasy. All successful people, from billionaire financiers to heart surgeons, start out with a *vision* of what they want to do. The stronger the vision, the greater their chances of seeing it through.

If possible, prepare yourself by using a deep relaxation technique to set your intuitive powers in motion. Then visualize yourself working in an ideal setting:

➠ *What* are you doing?
➠ *Where* are you?
➠ *Who* are you with?

What did you see? Was it of a specific or general nature? Were you doing one job or several? Were you indoors or out, moving around or stationary? Is your dream broadly in line with your other aspirations and capabilities, or do you need to think again?

Whatever the outcome, you are not finished yet. Record your findings in your portfolio, then move on to the next stage – research.

Research and Goal Setting

Once you have a direction in mind, no matter how general, it's time to get down to some serious study of what's happening out there in the careers arena. Whether or not you have access to a careers adviser, you must still be prepared to update your knowledge on an ongoing basis; your future depends on it.

There are already hundreds and hundreds of occupations listed in various guides, but none of these can ever be completely up-to-date. The world is changing rapidly, and new types of occupation are being created with equal speed. You will never be able to examine every option, but the more systematic your investigations, the better the results will be.

Before you begin, make sure you fully understand your objective. You already have some idea of the work you would really enjoy, whether as a single occupation or part of portfolio career.

Your next task is to match your dreams to reality by exploring occupational areas, specific professions and organizations. After that, you will narrow these down to options that are worth following up further. This process will continue until you have some firm goals in mind, such as booking training or embarking on a job-search campaign. Alternatively, if you have no immediate plans to move on, you can simply record your findings for future reference.

To help with the refining process, before you add a prospect to your shortlist, ask yourself some questions. For instance:

⮕ What would this work really be like and how would I feel about doing it?
⮕ How does it fit in with my personal life, values and leisure interests?
⮕ Do I already have the right skills and qualifications or could I acquire them?
⮕ Will it generate sufficient income for my needs?
⮕ What is the outlook for this occupation/sector/industry – growth or decline?
⮕ What are the opportunities for professional development?

Aim to come up with a list of at least three possibilities, then rank them in order of preference. Go for your ideal first, but don't lose sight of the others. If you find that the most attractive options are out of your reach for the time being, keep the details in your file for possible action at a later date.

Don't reject temporary work out of hand; it may give you new skills and lead on to better things. If your immediate need is for money to survive, then a less than perfect job is better than none. Settling for a compromise solution at this stage does not exclude the possibility of realizing your dreams at a later date. Look at your 'survival' job as a stepping stone, and continue to research better alternatives.

Your research can take any shape or form, but here are some tried and tested methods to choose from:

Use your Contact List

This is an ideal time to put your contact list to use, and start talking to people. Gather information from those you already know, and use the methods below to identify new contacts. If necessary, go back and read Chapter Seven again. From now on, *networking* should be at the forefront of all your efforts.

Explore Internet Resources

The amount of help and guidance available on the Internet is too vast to cover in detail here, but in Appendix Two you will find a list of useful sites to get you started, plus details of books that will help you to exploit its resources to the full.

In the meantime, let's have a brief look at on-line interest inventories. Although these are best used as part of a guidance session with a career management consultant, they can give you some very useful pointers if you don't have access to professional help. They work by helping you to match your interests and preferences to occupational fields and jobs, and are often used to stimulate further discussion with advisers. However, the results should never be interpreted in isolation, but used as part of the broader considerations we have already explored.

It's also important to remember that the Internet carries a large amount of unregulated material, so always check the source of anything you access. Likewise, bear in mind that some services will be free and others chargeable.

Many of the resources available at libraries can also be accessed on the Internet, with the advantage that you will be getting the very latest intelligence via company, agency and newspaper websites.

Exploit Library Resources

Local and reference libraries offer a wealth of information and guidance material. Below are some of the resources available:

Books containing sample psychometric and aptitude tests – very useful ways to find out more about yourself in relation to prospective careers. These type of assessments are also frequently used by recruiters, so familiarizing yourself with them serves a dual purpose.

A–Z guides – these vary in size, some listing thousands of occupations. Fortunately, there are also more condensed versions, averaging about 350 entries, and these are certainly more user-friendly for beginners. Start by casting your eye over the index, then, if you see something of interest, go to the relevant information page. There you should find an outline of the work involved in any particular occupation, together with details of training and qualifications needed, personal qualities sought, starting salaries and where to get further information.

A wide variety of newspapers and professional/trade journals – check the advertised vacancies to see what jobs are available and the skills and qualifications required. Read news items to spot opportunities, such as a new company coming to town. Many newspapers also have dedicated careers sections, with highly informative articles on trends in the job market, and information about career-planning seminars and workshops. Financial publications can be equally useful.

Guides for special communities, such as school leavers, graduates, people in their middle years and executives

Promotional material for government-funded initiatives

Telephone directories and Yellow Pages

Business directories – these will allow you to investigate organizations in different ways, for instance, by industry or location

Training directories and college prospectuses

Lists of the top-rated companies

Labour market reviews

Details of recruitment agencies

Magazines and journals devoted to careers information

Access to on-line information (check first; this may not be available at all libraries)

Guides to using the Internet

There is also a variety of books you can borrow, exploring career development and job search from every conceivable angle. None of these will ever be completely current, but they can still offer some extremely helpful guidance. Always make sure you get the latest edition available.

Send for Company Reports and Brochures

Annual reports and other publications can give you a valuable insight into an organization's performance, policies, markets and ethics. In this way you can make comparisons between, for example, working in the public sector or for a multinational corporation. Alternatively, you may find smaller companies to your taste. Some establishments will also have graduate recruitment brochures, which tell you exactly what careers are available and what qualities and qualifications are sought. If you are not a graduate, don't be afraid to phone and ask for a brochure; it may give a clue to other openings within the company.

Attend Careers and Trade Fairs/Exhibitions

This is an excellent way to meet company representatives and recruiters face to face. Things can move very fast at these events, so make sure you go armed with business cards, CVs and some relevant questions. You may even be put through a mini-interview, so think about this ahead of time.

Look around You

Learn to make your own estimation of possible openings and trends by staying alive to what's happening in the world around you. As you will see from the following examples, it doesn't always require special expertise to predict growth areas.

As technology advances and the world shrinks, the *communications* industry grows ever more important. Opportunities are spiralling, not only for computer specialists, but for marketing professionals and other creative types who are able to help organizations promote their products and services. Just switch on the television or pick up a magazine to see the amount of effort that goes into promoting company brands. All of this means jobs.

We are all becoming far more inventive and selective about what we do in our spare time, which is why the *leisure* industry is expanding so rapidly. This means more jobs in hotels, sports centres, health clubs, travel and tourism. The work is often part-time or self-employed, which may fit in well with a portfolio career.

When companies shed permanent staff and rationalize their operations, the need for expertise in certain areas is often met by an increased use of *consultants*. This can be in any area of the business, from IT and training to marketing and design. It may involve joining a consultancy firm or, if you have the expertise, setting up on you own.

Therapists and *counsellors* are in huge demand in an increasingly stressful world. Practitioners are often self-employed, enjoying flexible working patterns which allow them to set their own timetable.

If security is your priority, and you have the aptitude, you might want to consider a career in the *law* or *accountancy*. These professions are likely to survive even the gloomiest economic conditions. The same goes for the *medical profession*, although you may find working conditions and pay in the public sector less to your liking. Alternatively, look for occupations where there is a severe skills shortage, such as *engineering*. However, be aware that *manufacturing* can take a severe battering when there is a downturn in the economy.

Every day you are seeing people engaged in rewarding occupations, but they may not be registering as potential jobs for you. In future, as you are out and about, watching TV or socializing, stay alert to what other people are doing for a living, and make a note to research anything that might be suitable for you.

Careers Advisers and Consultants

Not surprisingly, many people find it difficult to navigate their way through the maze of information and guidance available, particularly at the first attempt. This is why you should make maximum use of any free services available, whether in the shape of a college adviser, government-sponsored initiative for the unemployed or company-financed outplacement programme. As time goes by, you will become increasingly self-sufficient, but nothing can equal having a personal adviser on hand the first time round. As well as giving you one-to-one counselling, they may also have group training sessions, computer programs to help with career choices and staff who are qualified to administer psychometric tests.

Alternatively, you can hire an independent careers consultant. These are different from recruitment consultants in that their primary aim is not to act as a placement agency, but to help you acquire the knowledge and skills to manage your own career. They may have a recruitment arm attached, but initially they should offer an impartial assessment and guidance service. It will cost you money, but could prove a good investment in the long run. Services range from CV preparation to comprehensive career planning and job-search support. A full programme could cost you thousands, so minimize the charges by first doing as much as possible on your own. If you do sign up, always ensure that objectives and payments are agreed in writing.

Consultancies range from individual practitioners to large organizations, and services vary. There is no overall regulatory body, but most practitioners agree to work to the specific codes of conduct laid down by their professional associations. These include the International Association of Career Management Professionals and the International Board for Career Management Certification (as its names implies, the latter also

arranges accreditation for suitably experienced professionals).
National bodies include the UK's Institute of Personnel
Development and the Australian Association of Career
Counsellors Inc.

Another way to assess expertise is to ask about success rates. If
a consultancy is doing well, it should be proud to offer you evidence of its achievements.

Self-employment

As job security erodes, more and more people are turning to self-employment as a way to regain control over their own destiny.
Although it has many attractions, make no mistake, working for
yourself is a tough assignment. As well as having talent in your
chosen field, you must be prepared for involvement in book-keeping, marketing and customer service. You will also need
great stamina, creativity, and all the other qualities covered in the
preceding chapters.

Nonetheless, many individuals are successfully setting up their
own businesses, and most of them would find it very difficult to
return to salaried work. For them, the advantages of operating
independently far outweigh the risks involved.

Having pondered the above, if you still like the idea of being
your own boss, here are some more points to consider:

➡ Research your market. A good idea is not enough. You need to
find out who wants your product or service.
➡ Get as much professional advice as you can, whether from a
bank, accountant or government-sponsored business advice
service.
➡ Prepare a basic business plan. This will give your idea substance and help you to get any necessary finance.
➡ Let your friends, family and business contacts know what you
are doing. You will need all the support you can get.
➡ Check whether you need professional indemnity insurance.
➡ Think about arranging your own pension and life insurance
cover.

Lifelong Learning

The promotion of lifelong learning for individuals is a subject of increasing study by governments, industry and academics. This stems from the realization that the business world needs an ever more educated, flexible and multi-skilled workforce. But who is going to oversee the process of continuous development when people are moving between jobs on an unprecedented scale?

Various think-tanks continue to debate the issue, but a subject of such complexity will not be resolved overnight. Whatever the experts conclude, at the end of the day no one is better placed to take charge of your growth than you yourself. *Learning* is not just about studying or being trained; it is about observation, curiosity and insight. Educators and trainers can certainly point you in the right direction, but ultimately these are qualities that you must nourish in yourself.

Naturally, you will want to take advantage of any training provided by employers, but you must be ready to mastermind your own progress by continuously putting your development needs to the test. If necessary, you will have to make independent arrangements to fill any gaps in your skills bank. However, before parting with any cash, make sure the training will have a measurable impact on your career. Choosing the wrong course can be an expensive mistake in terms of money and time.

This is a good opportunity to start thinking about your future learning needs, so use the following to help you plan ahead. If necessary, come back to the exercise when you have done some more research into prospective occupations.

Use the following broad headings as a guide, and subdivide them to suit your own situation.

Qualifications

Academic ....

Professional ....

Skills
Occupational ....

Interpersonal ....

Where skills are concerned, you will find that *computer literacy* is essential for nearly all jobs. Information technology is used across the workplace, not just in offices. Strong written and verbal *communication skills* are equally prized and fluency in one or more foreign languages is becoming more important as organizations expand their global operations.

Once you have identified your needs, stage two is to think about how and where you will acquire your learning. This will vary according your individual circumstances, but will no doubt include some of the methods listed below:

☐ employer courses – some recruitment agencies may also offer free help, particularly when it comes to cross-training on computer systems

☐ University, college and adult education courses – full or part-time, including evening classes

☐ Government initiatives

☐ Distance learning, including on-line and correspondence courses

☐ Professional associations and chambers of commerce services

☐ Professional training organizations
☐ Private tuition on a one-to-one basis
☐ Self-study using books, the Internet or computer packages
☐ Work experience or voluntary work

Once you have identified a possibility, it can be investigated in more detail by using the same research methods as before.

As for the broader aspects of learning, this is a matter of watching what other people do, getting feedback on your own performance, and analysing your experiences. It means always staying on the alert for opportunities, and leaving yourself open to new ideas.

Make sure you keep a record of all the qualifications and skills you acquire. This is not simply a matter of making lists and filing certificates, but of keeping thank-you letters, press clippings and any other evidence of achievement.

Time for Action

As you can see, managing your own career is not limited to finding a suitable occupation. It's about getting in touch with who you really are, and ensuring that you maintain your employability through an ongoing process of research, evaluation and distillation. Being able to give expression to your talents through a fulfilling working life is a dream that can be achieved, but it requires energy, enthusiasm and the strictest application of time management principles.

SUMMARY

* To succeed in the new world of work you must develop career resilience.
* Accept that you are likely to work in a range of roles and sectors, and build up your skills base accordingly.
* Keep abreast of trends and opportunities; your future depends on it.
* Get to know yourself well and use your intuitive powers to help you set goals.

* Ensure your continued employability by making a firm commitment to lifelong learning.

Chapter Nine

Your CV (Résumé)

A CV is not a list of jobs, but a powerful piece of advertising material.

Basic Guidelines

Your CV is a highly important sales document. Its purpose is to get you an interview, and to do that it must persuade the recipient that you have got what it takes to do the job. You may be competing with hundreds, even thousands, of other applicants, so it must demonstrate your abilities in a way that will grab your potential employer's attention and ensure that you stand out from the competition.

The CV is the one and only aspect of the selection process where you are in complete control, and the results you get will be in direct proportion to the amount of effort you put into its preparation. You will find no shortage of opinions and guidance as to what constitutes a 'winning' document, but let's look first at some basic guidelines:

➡ Keep information simple and concise.

➡ Avoid jargon and expressions that may not be understood.

➡ Write in the third person (as if you were describing someone else), so that you can highlight achievements without appearing egotistical. This is the standard approach and it also adds authority to what you say.

➡ Don't just list responsibilities – emphasize how you got results, for instance, by winning new business, controlling budgets, making cost savings, introducing new ideas – show how you made a difference. Quantify what you have done by using precise facts and figures. For instance 'boosted sales by 25 per cent' paints a far better picture than 'substantially increased sales'.

➡ Use a word processor to create a professional image and a document that can be tailored to specific applications.

➡ Choose good quality white paper – coloured paper produces poor photocopies (copies of CVs are often passed around within the company). For the same reason, don't put it in a binder. ·

➡ Use a quality printer and, if you send out photocopies, a good copier. Never compromise on this; go to a print shop if necessary.

➡ Use bold type for emphasis, but avoid overuse of fancy fonts and italics which may detract from your central message.

➡ Make the layout attractive and easy to read, with a mix of standard text and bullets.

➡ Use strong, positive verbs to demonstrate how you got results – for example:

achieved	created
implemented	increased
overhauled	regenerated
exceeded	generated
launched	managed
resolved	solved

➡ Aim for two pages at the most and make sure the most important details are on page one.

➡ Be positive, but don't lie – if you get an interview or undergo tests, it's likely that any inconsistencies will be spotted. Employers are getting wise to false claims made on CVs, so don't include anything you can't back up when you meet face to face. Some organizations may even use pre-employment screening (PES) companies, who specialize in weeding out fraudsters and embellishers.

⇒ Check carefully for spelling mistakes, and, if possible, get someone else to proofread and comment on the finished article.

The Format

The standard CV format is 'reverse chronological', where you detail your most recent jobs and experience first. However, if you have a long and varied job history, or are aiming for a career change, it might be better to put your key skills and *relevant* experience in an additional section ahead of the career summary. No one wants to wade through quantities of superfluous information before getting to the essential details. On the other hand, if you have no work experience at all, this approach allows you to highlight other abilities. The golden rule is to make it easy for the reader to decide that you are worth interviewing; before committing anything to paper, always ask yourself how it will look to the other side.

Here are suggested layouts for each of these approaches:

Reverse Chronological Format

1   Your name, address and telephone number.

2   A short description of yourself, called a **profile,** which gives the reader a snapshot of who you are and what you can do. This is usually three to four lines long.

3   Your **career history** or **work experience**, emphasizing your achievements in relation to what your potential employer is looking for. Put your most recent job first, then work backwards. On the whole, organizations will be more interested in your most recent experience, so summarize

anything you did more than ten years ago, unless it is of special relevance to the targeted job. Help them to form a picture of you by giving examples of how you brought about tangible benefits.

4   **Education and Qualifications** should be kept brief, with school results omitted if you have a substantial career behind you or have acquired more relevant credentials in the meantime. Include any appropriate training courses you have attended, even if they did not result in a diploma or certificate. (Recent graduates and school leavers are different. Employers will be more interested in your education, so it can be shown before the work details. Course work and projects can also be outlined if they have a bearing on the target job. If grades are not good, leave them out.)

5   **Interests** can add zest and help to highlight qualities that may not be revealed elsewhere. For instance, captaining a sports team may show that you have leadership potential, or organizing community events could indicate project-management abilities. Sports or other physical pursuits also suggest that you are fit and healthy (even if you're not). If your pastimes are less compelling, see if you can make them more salesworthy. For instance, 'reading' sounds terminally dull, but 'reading biographies' injects a sense of purpose.

6   Apart from your name, address and telephone number, **personal details**, including your date of birth, should be left to the end, perhaps in a section headed **Additional Information**. Here you can also include other marketable details, such as articles you have written or community activities. If you feel that your date of birth will count against you, I would suggest that you create your own 'equal opportunity', by leaving it out. In the UK, some careers consultants consider that such an omission will be

noticed, but in my experience if the rest of the CV is strong enough it will still entice the employer to see you. The same goes for omitting marital status, number of children and nationality. The exception to this is where such details have been specifically requested.

Key Skills and Experience Format

This is a format with obvious advantages for the new breed of 'career resilient' professional, including those building up a portfolio career.

The main difference between this and the standard format is that you add a 'Key Skills and Experience' (or similar) section before going into a briefer career history. Here you first highlight any capabilities that can be *transferred* to the job you are seeking. For instance, managers are often involved in staff development, which might qualify them for a new career in training. Likewise, a woman returning to the labour market could use her experience of raising a family to bring out financial and diary management skills (to name but a few).

If you are a graduate or school leaver, this section could cover accomplishments at school or university, such as editing a magazine or directing plays. Depending on the position you are aiming for, these activities may be just as relevant to an employer as the degree you get. Turning out a popular magazine may position you well for a future in journalism or publishing, but the creative talent and discipline involved would be equally appreciated in any number of commercial organizations. It also demonstrates a mastery of office technology and strong written communication skills, both absolutely vital when it comes to producing powerful reports and eye-catching presentations. Directing the school play may not launch you into a theatrical career, but you could use the experience to demonstrate project- and people-management skills.

If you have been out of work, and are unable to account for your time with other meaningful pursuits, the format also gives you the opportunity to omit periods of unemployment by first drawing attention to your achievements, then, in the career history section, listing employers and job titles without dates. For example:

Marketing Manager – Walker's Widgets	3 years
Sales Executive – Prestige Products	2 years

The missing dates could well raise questions, but, again, if the overall CV is interesting enough, it may still win you an interview. When other possibilities have been exhausted, an unorthodox approach is always worth a try. The interview itself is a different matter; there you will have to acknowledge the facts, but doing this in person gives you far more scope to use your powers of persuasion, something we will examine in Chapter Eleven.

Other Formats

There are many variations on the above themes, and it will come as no surprise that there are a number of books on the subject. You can also buy computer packages that will take you through the preparation process step by step, giving a choice of layouts and example paragraphs. And of course there are Internet sites that will help you do much the same.

What to Leave Out

As well as the personal details already discussed, there are other things that are usually left out of the CV, such as:

➡ Photographs, which can create a negative bias for any number of reasons.

➡ Current salary – this can be discussed at the interview, where you can use the negotiating skills outlined in Chapter Five.

➡ References – the employer will usually ask for referees before making a final offer, so leave it to them.

➡ Health details, unless you think they will work to your advantage.

- Disability. Don't invite prejudice – any special arrangements can be discussed if and when you are invited to an interview.

- Reasons for leaving your last employment.

- Poor examination results – better to leave them out than show poor grades. Always aim to give a totally positive impression.

- Addresses of previous employers.

- Months of employment – years are enough, for example, 1992–1999.

- Certificates, diplomas, press clippings, thank-you letters or any other testimonials. This will be viewed as junk mail, only increasing the likelihood of your application ending up in the waste bin.

However, if you are responding to an advertised vacancy which specifically requests a photograph or other omitted details, you will have to supply them.

Computer Screening

If you think it's a safe bet that the first screening of your CV will be done by a human being, think again. Computer programs, which can select or reject your carefully completed document in a matter of seconds, are fast replacing personnel staff as the first stage in the selection process, particularly for large companies which are inundated with responses to advertised vacancies.

So how can you convince the computer that you are good enough to go through to the next round, where a human will decide whether or not you are short-listed for interview? Fortunately, if you follow the above guidelines, you can't go far wrong. The secret lies in keeping the information simple and concise, paying attention to the layout and including the words that correspond to the knowledge and key skills the recruiter is looking for.

The more basic programs work by searching for key words, such as the office technology used in the job. More advanced systems sift candidates by identifying specific skills or levels of responsibility. In either case, failure to use the right terminology means that your application will never reach the personnel department or other relevant staff. Unlike their human counterparts, computers are unlikely to make allowances for even the smallest errors, so make it a habit to double-check everything you do.

Example CVs

Whether or not you plan to do some further study on the subject, this is an ideal time to sketch out a basic document for yourself, using the information you have assembled in earlier chapters. It may help to take a look at the example skeleton CVs which follow. These are based on the work records and interests of real candidates, although certain details have been changed to protect confidentiality and reinforce learning points. To demonstrate how the approach can vary according to the individual's situation, a mature career changer has been contrasted with a recent graduate. The final versions would be modified, or fleshed out, to suit the specific job or assignment in question.

Although both documents are structured within a conventional framework, you will see that there is still scope for flexibility in exactly how the information is presented. There are no absolute rules, and you are just as free to manipulate your own details in a way that shows your talents to the best advantage.

The examples used are British, but on the whole they would work equally well in America. The main difference is that, because of the tighter equality legislation, the exclusion of personal details on an American résumé would not be questioned.

Example A – Career Changer CV

CAROL CHANGER
22 Oxford Road
London SW6 RJU
0171 XXX XXXX

Training consultant with seven years' experience in the private and public sectors. Proven ability to design and deliver innovative courses and workshops across the personal development spectrum.

KEY SKILLS AND EXPERIENCE

– Devised and led successful pilot 'People Management' Workshop for the Metropolitan Police Service, resulting in the sale of a series of further training courses for Inspectors.

– Designed and delivered an award-winning programme of Professional Development training for students throughout West London.

– Wrote and implemented a range of Communication Skills and Time Management workshops for secretarial and customer support staff at Blue Chip Limited.

– Produced and directed video on Customer Care Techniques. Wrote and illustrated accompanying workbook.

– Trained executive staff in use of new office technology, including e-mail and electronic diary management.

– Organized a series of management development seminars for teachers and lecturers which won the National Industry and Education Partnership award for Quality and Innovation in Training.

CAREER HISTORY

Blue Chip Limited, West London

1997 – 1999 **Publishing Department Team Leader – Consultancy Services Division**

– Set up and managed a team of five professionals with responsibility for in-house production of flyers, brochures and other marketing material.

1992 – 1997 **Office Services Supervisor/Community Affairs Representative**

– Supervised and trained 30 secretarial and reception staff.
– Organized training initiatives for colleges and other organizations in the local community.

1988 – 1992 **Executive Secretary**

Previous Employment: Includes 2 years as a Sales Person for Voyages Français, Paris and 3 years as an Administrator for Platinum Pharmaceuticals plc, London W1.

TRAINING AND QUALIFICATIONS

- National Vocational Qualification (NVQ) – Level 4 Trainers' Award
- Certificate in Counselling Skills – Central School of Counselling and Therapy
- 'Train the Trainers' Certificate – Blue Chip Limited
- Successfully completed a wide range of personal and professional development courses

INTERESTS

Tennis, Yoga and Interior Design
Volunteer Teacher of English to Speakers of Other Languages

Example B – Graduate CV

GARY GRADUATE
22 Caledonian Avenue
Kingston upon Thames
Surrey KT1 2AB
0181 XXX XXXX

Resourceful graduate with significant commercial experience gained in pre-university employment with a multinational IT company. Accustomed to working on own initiative and able to interact effectively with people at all levels, from a wide variety of backgrounds.

EDUCATION

1998 BSc (Hons) 2.1, Economics – Wellknown University

WORK HISTORY

1994 – 1995 **Big Systems International Limited**, Central London
Business Support Assistant – Government Sales

Member of a small team providing campaign and administrative support to 30 Account Managers and Sales Professionals:

- Conducted customer satisfaction surveys and exhibited at major trade exhibitions.
- Provided telephone guidance to customers and maintained marketing database.

- Used a range of PC software to transform complex data into charts and graphs readily understood by customers.
- Assisted with production of reports and contracts, including research of data and compilation of statistics.
- On own initiative, streamlined unit's on-line central filing system and compiled quick reference user's guide.
- Revitalized internal communications by introducing and editing a newsletter for staff based in diverse locations around the country.
- Achieved top rating in performance appraisal in recognition of personal contribution to unit's 30% increase in sales.

Summer Work

1997	**The Happy Nappy Company** – Sydney, Australia Packed nappy supplies
	Young Diary Projects – Brisbane, Australia Telesales professional – sold advertising space in school diaries
1996	**Summer Camp** – North Carolina, USA Supervised ten 6–14-year-olds and taught rifle shooting
1995	**Harridges** – London Sales Assistant and Karaoke Demonstrator – Toy Department

ADDITIONAL INFORMATION

Interests: Football, rafting and chess. Maintown Women's Football Team Coach.
Date of Birth: 4 September 1976
Software: Proficient in Excel, Word, Power Point and Lotus 1–2–3

Now let's look at the rationale behind each of these documents:

A – The Mature Career Changer

The 'Key Skills and Experience' section appears before the reverse chronological career history because Carol is aiming to move from a variety of support and supervisory roles to a career as a freelance trainer. The CV is designed for approaches to training organizations, but she would also have a flyer or brochure for marketing her services to corporate clients and members of the public.

Carol has never held a formal training position or worked in a Human Resources role. Her seven years' relevant experience has been gained largely as a result of on-the-job training of reporting staff and in the voluntary role of Community Affairs Representative for Blue Chip Limited. This has not been highlighted on the CV, but could be discussed at interview.

Note the use of 'action' words at the beginning of each bullet:

devised designed wrote produced
trained organized set up supervised.

As a forty-five-year-old, Carol has decided to omit her date of birth and some of the earlier employment from a career spanning 28 years. However all *relevant* details have been included.

She is not a graduate, and until recently had no formal qualifications other than school examinations. This is not a barrier because her work history far outweighs her lack of academic achievement. The NVQ qualification has been earned by demonstrating on-the-job competence, and the counselling certificate from an evening class course.

If she decides to supplement her income with secretarial work, a separate CV would show her secretarial experience first, with the other roles summarized. The training qualification would also be taken out in case it made her seem over-qualified.

B – Young Graduate

Gary is a recent graduate aiming for a career involving Information Technology, preferably in a role providing business solutions to customers.

At this stage in his life, the degree is a major selling point so it is shown first. As time goes by, it would be relegated to a later section of the CV.

He already has an impressive work history, so this is emphasized in favour of achievements at university. Most employers appreciate candidates with some business exposure. A graduate with a less-marketable commercial record, or a degree related directly to his or her chosen profession, could add an 'achievements' (or similar) section to elaborate on course work or college projects. Gary could do the same if he identified other activities that *added value* to his application.

He uses the profile to demonstrate maturity and interpersonal skills, anticipating that companies value self-reliance and good communication as much as academic success.

Powerful verbs are employed to convey his energetic approach to work and demonstrate how he made a significant *difference* to the department's performance, such as, 'streamlined', 'revitalized', 'achieved'. This shows someone who has transformed a modest role into something special by his own efforts. Similar 'action' words would be equally effective in describing social, community or voluntary accomplishments.

Age is a good selling point, so the date of birth is included.

Gary's technical experience is limited, but his solution-driven approach and ability to handle complex information are equally strong selling points. As a graduate recruit, he could expect appropriate technical training.

The summer jobs bring a touch of light relief, as does Gary's coaching role. Sifting through CVs can be a tedious business, so everything else being equal, recruiters might just be tempted to invite him to an interview to find out more about the nappy (diaper) company, the karaoke demonstrations and how he became involved with a women's football team.

Overseas experience is a good selling point. Many companies are competing in a global arena, and they value staff who appreciate cross-cultural issues. It also demonstrates initiative and a pioneering spirit, both highly transferable skills.

The CV will be sent to a variety of companies in the medium to large range, particularly those actively seeking graduates. However, many organizations with graduate recruitment schemes prefer to issue application forms, something that will be covered in the next chapter.

Action

Now that you understand the theory behind the process,

schedule some time in your diary to work on your own core CV (or CVs). Remember, this is about writing a persuasive sales document, so be generous with the time you allow. It is not a question of writing a list, but of creating powerful advertising material, an exacting business for anyone.

If you find yourself suffering from writer's block, use a deep relaxation technique to release your intuition. Get your ideas down in any way you like, making maximum use of colour, pictures and diagrams. Don't slow yourself down at this stage by worrying about grammar or style. Just work on capturing the essence of what you want to express. Over time, ideas will start to flow of their own accord, often coming to the surface when you least expect it, so make sure you keep a supply of pens and paper around the house. Experiment with different presentations until you find your own definitive style.

Once you have an acceptable first draft, you can start the process of refinement. Be prepared to make several attempts before you produce the finished article. If you have any doubt about the wisdom of spending so much time on this exercise, just think about the transferable skills you are developing. Commercial reports, proposals and presentations all demand exactly the same type of creative effort.

When it comes to customizing your document for specific positions and organizations, the acid test is 'would this entice an employer to see me?' To get a meaningful answer, you will have to put yourself in the recipient's place by doing your homework on the targeted company and job.

If the end result is lacking in dynamism, could it be sending you a message about your life in general? There is no doubt that employers prefer people who are *involved* and interesting. Stylish packaging can enhance your presentation, but it is no substitute for solid experience. Could you be using your time more productively, even if it means taking on some charity work or enrolling on a course? There may be no need to make dramatic changes in your routine; just two or three hours a week can work wonders.

If you really don't have the time or capability to come up with a polished document at this stage, there is always the option of getting professional help. There are a number of ways to do this, but make thorough investigations before parting with any money. Newspapers and magazines carry numerous advertisements for companies offering a 'professional CV service', but don't take anything on trust. They may well be able to produce an attractive layout, but do they have the expertise to come up with a vibrant sales document? You now have sufficient knowledge to ask informed questions, so make use of it.

Careers consultants and advisers, whether independent or government-funded, usually include CV preparation as part of their overall services. Recruitment consultants and employment agencies may also offer help, but they often use methods tailored to their own unique way of selling your skills. Don't reject anything out of hand, but always ask for explanations, and never accept anything you are uncomfortable with. No one else can ever be an expert on *your* life, and it is *you* who will have to do the explaining at the interview.

Getting people to talk about their accomplishments can be like extracting teeth, so a reputable consultant will welcome any preparatory work you do. Even taking along a list of achievements and dates of employment can make a big difference. It also cuts down on the time you spend with them, which in turn reduces any fees involved.

Whether you compile it yourself or use a professional service, the CV is not a static document, but something that will evolve along with your experience. You may not always have time for regular updates, but keep notes in your portfolio so that changes can be incorporated when needed. Job advertisements tend to reflect the latest trends in terminology, so keep an eye open for phrases that could add some sparkle to your text. The underlying principles never change, but fashions of presentation come and go. Technology will also be a major influence on the CV of the future, so keep in touch with developments.

Of course, once you have a CV, you will need to know how to use it. It will only work as part of a structured job-search strategy, something we will look at in the next chapter.

SUMMARY

* The only successful CV is the one that gets you an interview.
* To be an effective sales document it must be simple and concise, but powerful in terms of action words that demonstrate how you get results.
* There are a range of styles and formats that can be tailored to your individual circumstances.
* The skills developed in creating your document can also be put to use in writing reports, proposals and presentations.
* If the finished product is lacking in dynamism, it may be sending you a message about your life in general.

Chapter Ten

Your Job-search Campaign

Finding a job is a job in itself,
deserving all the time and
attention you would give to any
other professional assignment.

Getting the job or assignment you really want is like launching a
new product. To achieve the best results you will need a structured campaign plan. Viewing the process as a business project
will also take the emotion out of the exercise, particularly when it
comes to coping with rejection.

The first step is to develop the right mind-set, which means
believing in your product, knowing what you want and going all
out to get it. Indulging in self-doubt will only slow you down, so
tell yourself: 'There are people out there who *need my skills*, and
I'm going to find them.' You will then be ready to streamline your
plan of attack by:

➡ setting up a campaign base
➡ budgeting for expenses
➡ identifying job prospects and making approaches
➡ setting targets and measuring your progress

Your Campaign Base

If you are going to be operating from home, start by finding a
work room and clear some space for a 'campaign corner'.
Getting a job is a job in itself, and allocating a designated work
area will help to remind you of this. Try to keep the room light
and airy, and use fresh flowers or plants to enliven the

atmosphere and encourage the flow of energy. If setting up at home is difficult, make the most of library or college facilities. Whether at home or via outside services, you will also need access to a variety of equipment and supplies such as:

- A word processor or personal computer. If you really can't get access to either a typewriter will do.
- Access to the Internet (optional).
- A telephone, preferably with an answerphone or other message-taking service. If your campaign goes well, you can expect lots of calls.
- A fax machine (some companies may be in a hurry to see your details).
- A good quality photocopier.
- Stationery, stamps and business cards.
- Directories, newspapers and magazines.

Budgeting for Expenses

Naturally the above will involve a certain amount of expense. Add to this the cost of phone calls, electronic communications and travel, and you will see how important it is to make forecasts and keep track of your spending. If your image needs a boost, you may also have to plan for new clothes and grooming. When finances are tight, thinking ahead will help you to extend the scope of your activities and make trade-offs where necessary.

For those of you facing redundancy or already out of work, company outplacement centres or government schemes can provide a cost-effective alternative to 'going it alone', at least for the first few months. Facilities vary, but with luck, you may find yourself with access to all the necessary supplies and services, totally free of charge.

Identifying Prospects and Making Approaches

Identifying prospects is much the same as researching career opportunities, with the difference that, having decided on an occupation, you now need to pin down a potential employer or client. As we have seen, leads can come from a wide range of sources, but for the purposes of your campaign, let's group them into five broad categories:

- networking
- advertised vacancies
- speculative approaches
- agencies
- advertising your skills/capabilities

Networking

The very best way to start your job search is by talking to the people on your contact list. Unless they are good friends or family, let them know that you are in the market for work, but don't press them for leads or ask outright for a job. You are more likely to meet with a positive response if you keep the whole business on a casual basis, and simply ask if they can spare, say, twenty minutes, to give you some advice.

When you meet, be brief and concise in explaining your situation, then ask if there is any way they can help. Do they have any useful contacts or know of companies who are looking for staff? Could they keep an eye open for you? Can you mention their name when following up leads? Keep your questions tentative and polite, and whatever the outcome write a thank-you note afterwards.

Advisers often meet with resistance when they suggest networking as the first port of call, largely because so many job seekers feel uncomfortable about 'bothering' their contacts. This is sad, because most people are more than willing to help out if approached in the right way.

Advertised Vacancies

By contrast, the majority of candidates have no reservations at all about responding to suitable advertised vacancies. Obviously, this is a perfectly valid route to employment, but given that you

will probably be up against hordes of other applicants, it makes
sense to try other methods as well.

The great advantage to advertised vacancies is that they can be
found with ease, in any number of places, including:

- newspapers – national, local, community, ethnic and specialist
- trade journals
- graduate publications
- the Internet
- shop windows
- in-house company publications and notice-boards

Never rush into a response simply because the vacancy looks
vaguely suitable. So many people waste valuable time and effort
because they fail to analyse advertisements properly. This also
increases the likelihood of rejection, which in turns leads to
unnecessary disappointment and stress. It pays to go through the
advertisement very carefully, highlighting the key requirements,
and asking yourself, 'Can I really do this job right now?' Think,
too, about travel arrangements and any other aspects that are
important to you. If you still want the job, and can meet the *main*
criteria, go for it.

There may be a question mark over less crucial criteria, but
don't let this get in your way. For instance, one mature candidate
was put off by '*Young* company seeks Personal Assistant to work
for Managing Director'. Assuming that they were looking for
younger applicants, she had to muster all her courage to apply.
As it turned out, she got the job, beating ten other short-listed
candidates in the process. She also discovered that the company's
use of the term 'young' meant nothing more than 'newly formed'.
Moral? Never make assumptions.

In another instance, a job seeker thought that the company's
preference for a certain software package ruled him out, even
though he was proficient in a very similar application. Since he
was highly suitable in every other respect, I suggested he
explained the similarity in his covering letter, adding that he
would have no trouble adapting. The strategy worked, and he

was invited to an interview.

If the advertisement asks for a CV, try to send a version which has been tailored as far as possible to meet the demands of the job and the culture of the company. You will also need to write a covering letter, saying why you are applying and giving a brief summary of your main selling points. As with your CV, use good quality white paper and unless you are asked otherwise make sure the letter is typed. A handwritten communication may add a stylish personal touch, but only if you have superb handwriting and are sure that the company does not use a computer scanner. And don't let yourself down at this stage by neglecting to check for spelling mistakes and grammatical errors. If this is not your strong point, find someone else to help you.

What you write will depend on your personal circumstances and what the company is looking for, but the following example illustrates the basic principles involved. It relates to a young retail assistant looking for a step up the ladder into a supervisory role. He is answering a newspaper advertisement for retail supervisors for a large supermarket chain renowned for its commitment to quality products and customer service. The company is also offering successful candidates the chance to train for management roles. The applicant has analysed the company's requirements and highlighted the key points to be addressed in his response.

➡ sales or supervisory experience
➡ ambition and enthusiasm
➡ a desire to grow with an expanding, friendly organization

His letter takes account of these three essential requirements as follows:

Telephone no.

2 Grange Road
Bigtown
Grandshire
GR2 3BG

Ms Daljit Patel
Recruitment Officer
Quality Superstores
45 Main Street
Bigtown
Grandshire
GR7 8LG

4 June 1999

Dear Ms Patel,

Retail Supervisors – Your Reference: B123

You will see from the enclosed CV that my skills and experience match the requirements of the positions advertised in the *Chronicle* dated 3 June 1999.

For the last two years I have worked as a sales assistant at the Corner Minimarket, handling all aspects of the operation of a busy retail outlet. I am particularly proud of my contribution to a 20% increase in sales over the last year, arising largely from my introduction of special promotions and redesign of shelf and window displays.

My current ambition is to move into a supervisory role in an expanding organization such as Quality Superstores, where I can put my skills to profitable use in a friendly, customer-driven environment. Your training and development scheme would also give me the opportunity to achieve my longer-term goal of becoming a manager.

You can leave a message for me on the above number at any time, and I would be pleased to attend an interview to suit your convenience.

Your sincerely,

(Signature)

John Murphy

Note how the letter facilitates the decision-making process by:

⟹ Using a bold heading for instant identification of the position applied for

- Including the vacancy reference number – very important for large companies who may be advertising numerous positions at the same time
- Getting straight into the reason for applying
- Summarizing sales experience and demonstrating achievement of results
- Addressing the company's requirement for ambitious people looking for growth
- Balancing use of 'I' and 'me' with 'you' and 'yours' – more compelling for the recipient
- Using persuasive words like 'increase', 'profitable', 'busy'
- Subtly flattering company by acknowledging their customer-driven and friendly culture
- Making it easy for the company to contact/interview him
- Using the letter as a brief and concise attention-grabber – the CV will cover the detail

Many of my clients have used similar approaches to excellent effect, irrespective of their profession or level. Whether you are responding by external mail, fax or e-mail, the key points to remember are:

- explain where you saw the advertisement
- get straight to the point
- address the organization's specific requirements
- give a flavour of how you get results
- be brief, but persuasive

Make a note of the above points in your portfolio, and use it as a checklist each time you respond to an advertisement.

Of course, instead of asking for a CV, many companies prefer to use application forms. This is quite a different matter, and one that we shall cover more fully later in the chapter.

Speculative Approaches

Approaching an organization on the chance that they may have a job for you can, like networking, give you a significant competitive edge. Your letter may just arrive at the crucial point between a vacancy coming up and it being advertised. Some of my clients have even had posts created for them in response to a particularly timely approach. However, the more focused your enquiry, the better the results will be. This means:

➠ using your research skills to carefully 'target' organizations
➠ finding out who has the power to hire/interview you
➠ sending your CV and a covering letter

Identifying the appropriate decision-maker may take a few phone calls, but it plays a large part in determining the success of your efforts because a personalized letter is infinitely more persuasive than a communication starting with 'Dear Sir or Madam'.

When you phone, never say that you are looking for a job. The commercial world is full of 'guards', whose main purpose in life seems to be getting rid of job seekers in the shortest possible time. Always be one hundred per cent polite and positive, but make sure you are equally persistent. Say that you need to write to the person responsible for hiring staff, but don't be tempted to qualify your reasons any further. Better still, if it's a small company without the benefit of a Human Resources division, ask for the name of the manager or director of your targeted department.

Once you have a name, you are ready to write in much the same way that you would for an advertised vacancy. The main difference with a speculative letter is in the opening and closing paragraphs. Let's take the example of a senior manager with extensive experience of managing complex international projects. Having read in the press that a bank has plans for a major restructuring of its global operations, she writes along the following lines:

'I read in yesterday's *Times* that you are planning a major realignment of the bank's international operations, and thought that you might have a need for someone with my skills and experience.

During my 7 years with ABC International, I was accustomed to managing a variety of complex international projects, across a range of functions and lines of business. (*Continues to outline in 2–3 paragraphs how she can be of use to the target company.*)

Perhaps I could telephone you next week to discuss whether a meeting would be useful at this stage? In the meantime, I enclose my CV for your information.'

Note how the letter is designed to attract the recipient's interest without asking outright for a job. The question in the closing paragraph is of course rhetorical: 'Perhaps I could telephone you?' Of course, she *will* telephone, but framing her intention as a question avoids sounding too pushy, and keeps the power firmly in the hands of the recipient. Likewise, she keeps the process on a tentative basis by asking for a 'meeting', not an interview. This suggests a discussion between professionals, rather than a desperate approach from a job seeker.

So far, we have looked at *ideal* approaches, but not everyone has the time or skill to pin down decision-makers or to customize their CV and covering letter. For senior positions, you compromise at your peril, but for more modest posts, if you really have no other choice, don't despair. Candidates can sometimes get good results with a well-designed standard CV and covering letter, but it usually means casting the net very wide. The obvious disadvantage for someone financing their own job search is the cost of mailing such large numbers of letters.

At the other extreme, more confident and experienced individuals often take the option of telephoning their targeted recipient before sending a CV. They, too, can expect to encounter the guards, but a little diplomacy can work wonders in this respect. Secretaries, particularly at executive level, are paid to filter the boss's phone calls and re-direct as many as possible. Again, the technique is not to divulge your true purpose in calling, but simply to say that you must speak to the boss in person. If they still resist, try to get the secretary's name, and ask for her/his *advice* on the best time to phone again. This acknowledges their status and individuality, and can often tip the scales in your favour.

Once you have the necessary information, stop and think before you make the 'warm-up' call. Relax before you pick up the phone, and try standing up while you make the call. Believe it or not, this will strengthen your voice. Smiling will also help you to inject a more pleasant tone. Always have your CV in front of you, and highlight the major points that you would like to get across. Unless the other person is particularly keen to talk, keep the call brief; your main aim should be to get an agreement to send your CV, no more and no less. If you are told to contact someone else, ask if you can mention the referer's name by way of introduction.

If your approach is successful, the opening paragraph of your letter should refer to the phone call. For instance: 'Thank you for taking the time to speak to me today. As agreed, I enclose my CV for your consideration.'

Agencies and Recruitment Consultants

Recruitment agencies obviously play a key role in the job market, where the demand for contract and temporary staff is growing all the time. However, they can also help you to find permanent work, although once again, you will face competition. Whatever type of work you are looking for, if you do decide to use an agency as part of your campaign, look for firms that show a genuine interest in you as an individual. You can waste a great deal of time in following up unsuitable leads, so it pays to be selective.

To start with, you could register with just two or three well-established firms who specialize in the area you are interested in, then shop around for some personal recommendations. Clients have given me mixed feedback about agencies, but on the whole, the positive experiences outweigh the bad. Consultants may be dealing with hundreds of candidates, so the secret of success is to build up a strong rapport with your contact, and phone in regularly to remind them of who you are.

More and more recruitment firms are also advertising vacancies on the Internet, including overseas positions. Many also have the facility to e-mail fresh vacancies to clients on a regular basis. The good news for the 'unconnected' is that the Internet is still seen as an addition, rather than an alternative, to established recruitment methods.

Last, but not least, never reject state agencies such as Job Centres out of hand. Their expertise is growing all the time, particularly as they make increasing use of technology to search for vacancies or training opportunities. I have certainly seen some impressive results from this source. If in doubt, go along and have a look round.

Advertising Your Skills/Capabilities

For a comparatively small layout, you can take out a line advertisement in newspapers or trade/specialist journals. You can also use free Internet services by filling in a standard form which automatically creates a web page of information about you. Some of these sites (see Appendix Two), are well-known to recruitment consultants and employers, so your details have a reasonable chance of being seen, particularly if you are an IT professional or a graduate. However, before rushing to join the cyber-candidates, think about the reality of posting your life history for all the world to see. The Internet is well-known for its fringe activities, so anyone inviting you to an interview would have to be checked out very carefully. It is also advisable to keep personal details to a minimum.

If fact, the ways of advertising yourself are only limited by your imagination. Take the case of one unemployed forty-nine-year-old executive, whose unique publicity stunt was reported in the national press. Having given up on conventional job-search methods, he took to the road to advertise his availability. For two weeks he spent several hours a day standing on a highway verge, holding a placard saying, 'I need a job.' He was eventually spotted by the managing director of a local manufacturing firm, and landed the post of international sales manager. Not only that, he has since been head-hunted by dozens of other firms. This is a perfect example of how courage and determination, combined with a little inspiration, can turn even a seemingly hopeless situation into a resounding success story.

Application Forms

And now to the dreaded application form. Many employers prefer these to CVs because they allow the recruiters to dictate how your personal details and career history are presented. Gone are the days of the one-page form, as organizations put an increasingly greater premium on knowing exactly what makes you tick. In fact, in many cases you will find yourself with an application 'pack' that closely resembles an examination paper, except that it may take even longer to complete.

For the most part, you will have to provide whatever information is requested, with very little room for manoeuvre or omission. For instance, if asked for your date of birth and exam results, you are obliged to give them; ignoring any of the questions will probably mean instant rejection. However, where possible aim to be positive rather than negative, particularly when providing reasons for leaving. 'Reorganization' is more upbeat than 'redundancy', and 'for discussion at interview' is infinitely better than 'personality clash with manager'. (Yes, people really do write that!)

Providing factual answers is the easy part, even if they do sometimes reveal more than you would wish. The real test comes when completing the sections designed to fathom your portfolio of personal skills and/or problem-solving abilities. These can be very much like mini-interviews, and in fact are often used as the basis for further discussion at the interview. To get a flavour of how this works, take a look at the following, then think about the answers you might give. Your examples can be drawn from work, university, school or any other areas of your life.

- Describe a situation where you have taken charge; what were the main difficulties and how did you overcome them?
- Describe how you prioritized your workload in your last job (or at university/school etc).
- Can you give some examples of the equality issues we should consider when providing a reception service at the council's customer help desk?
- Is there anything else we should take into account when considering your application?

The first two are designed to test how you handle problems, and only you can provide the answers. However, the two last warrant some further discussion. As awareness of equality issues becomes more important it's a good idea to make sure you have some understanding of the subject, especially if you are looking for work in the public sector. Question three is designed to check how you would help to ensure equal access to services for diverse members of the community. You might, for example, be able to show the desirability of providing:

- wheelchair access
- information in community languages
- large-print brochures for people with a visual impairment
- interpreters

Question four, and others like it, are often left blank because candidates fail to recognize their importance. In fact, you should seize any such opportunity to market your skills on your own terms. This is the ideal place to include any special achievements or activities that might add value to your application, particularly if you have researched the organisation and can tailor your response to their specific operations and culture.

As you can see, the application form is just as much a sales document as your CV, so take the utmost care when completing it. Here are some points to watch out for:

- Give the application form as much care and attention as you would an examination paper.

- Before you start, read through the questions and any instructions/guidelines for completion.
- Take a photocopy of the blank form and use this to prepare your draft answers. This will help to avoid crossings-out or cramming.
- If you are using an on-line form, don't rush to key in the answers. First, make a note of the questions and prepare your answers carefully. Spelling mistakes and sloppy grammar are the scourge of electronic communications, and they *will* count against you.
- Don't include your CV unless specifically asked to do so.
- Take a photocopy of the final application or make a note of your on-line responses. If you succeed in getting an interview, you will need a record of exactly what you have told the organization.

And finally, don't be complacent about the 'informal' recruitment events held by large organizations, where you may be expected to fill in an application on the day. Selection is *never* an informal process, and you won't get a second chance if you screw up the first time round. Prepare carefully before you attend, and do some thorough research on the organization. You will no doubt be given a briefing presentation, so listen carefully and make notes. Take your CV along as a memory jogger, and make sure you are dressed for the part. In short, know why you are there and be prepared to make the maximum impact.

Targets and Follow-up

Good resolutions are all very well, but carrying them through is another matter. The best antidote for inertia is to set yourself targets and stick to them. It makes sense to use a mix of approaches, but you will have to decide for yourself what best suits your own circumstances. Make a note of your options then estimate which and how many you will attempt over a given timescale. You might want to use the following format:

Method	Number	By (date)
Speak to network contacts		
Make speculative approaches		
Respond to advertised vacancies		
Register with agencies		
Advertise in journals etc		

When it comes to targeting organizations for speculative approaches, draw up a 'hit list', then prioritize it. Check your diary in advance, and make sure you allow contingency time to cope with the unexpected. Exciting prospects can suddenly appear from nowhere, and interviews often happen at very short notice. A complex application form can take hours to complete, and a powerful CV even longer. You will also have to think about networking activities, when and where to do research, and any visits to appropriate agencies or consultants. Only the most careful time management will allow you to do everything you want, whilst still keeping information overload at bay.

Job search can be tiring, physically and emotionally. However, if you build in adequate time for deep relaxation, it can also be stimulating and enjoyable. Don't sacrifice your quiet time in the belief that other activities are more pressing at this stage. Even 30 minutes a day will pay huge dividends in the quality of your output, and hence the response you get from those who are able to help you.

You will also need to keep a job-search log, just as sales people record letters and visits to customers or prospects. Record whatever you think is important, but make sure you include the following for each approach:

Position applied for:
Name of organization:
Address:
Telephone number/Fax/E-mail (if appropriate):
Name of contact(s):
Source of application: for instance, speculative letter/network (name)/advertisement in …
Action/Date: sent CV 9.9.99
Comments: for instance, follow up by phone on 23.9.99 if nothing heard/Interview set for 30.9.99

Add further comments as the situation progresses.

Follow-up is extremely important. It's very tempting to mail a batch of letters, congratulate yourself on your efforts, then sit back and hope for the best. This is not a good idea for several reasons. Recruiters are extremely busy people, and there is always the chance that they will overlook you. Applications also get lost from time to time, and in yet other cases, the company may simply not have the capacity to reply to a huge number of applicants.

If, therefore, after allowing a respectable time, say two weeks, you have heard nothing, a discreet follow-up phone call is perfectly acceptable. Have your application in front of you, and be prepared to give all the necessary identifying details. That way if something has gone wrong you have the opportunity to put it right. Alternatively, you may be reassured that a reply will be coming soon. If it turns out that you have been unsuccessful you can move on to other things and possibly even get some useful feedback.

Lots of people feel very uncomfortable about making phone calls, for the simple reason that it can mean *instant* rejection. Forget about this; you haven't got time for such insecurities. If you need to make a call:

➡ prepare your 'script'
➡ take a deep breath
➡ smile and dial

Rejections come in many forms, some of them extremely amusing. But don't be disheartened if you receive the classic response: 'Your application has been unsuccessful this time, but your details are being kept on file.' This is not always just a gentle way of letting you down. Many people are astonished to be called to an interview within months, even weeks, of getting one of these letters.

If you succeed in getting an interview, send off an acceptance letter straight away, then clear some time to prepare yourself thoroughly.

SUMMARY

* Getting the job you really wants requires a structured campaign plan.
* Job leads come from five broad sources: networking; advertised vacancies; speculative approaches; agencies; self-advertising in journals or on the Internet.
* CVs should be accompanied by a brief, but persuasive covering letter.
* Application forms require the same care and attention you would give to a CV.
* Set yourself specific targets, keep a log of approaches and never neglect to follow up if you get no response.

Chapter Eleven

Interviews and other Selection Methods

It takes a matter of seconds for someone to form a first impression of you, so make every moment count.

Forward Planning

Most candidates view the prospect of a job interview with some trepidation. This is largely because they see the process as an interrogation, with all the hostile images that evokes. In fact, an interview is no more than a *discussion* between you and the recruiters. A position is vacant, and you are coming together to decide whether you are the best person to fill it. Seeing it from this perspective immediately takes a great deal of anxiety out of the situation, leaving you free to get on with the next big stress-buster – preparation.

Over the years I have had feedback from hundreds of interviewees, and there is no doubt that the difference between success and failure lies in careful forward planning. The recruiters won't leave anything to chance, so why should you? Whether you are an executive or just starting out at the bottom of the ladder, you will find that interviewers are applying ever more scientific techniques at all levels. It therefore follows that you must tackle the process with exactly the same degree of skill and discipline. Meet the challenge by drawing up a specific plan of action:

➡ fine tune your knowledge of the employer
➡ revisit your skills inventory

- rehearse possible questions and answers
- make a reconnaissance trip
- practise relaxation and visualization techniques
- devise a checklist of what to take with you

Knowledge is power at all stages of the selection process, but never more so than at the interview. You would never have got this far without doing some research, but now comes the time to make sure you have covered all the angles. For instance, do you know who will be doing the interview; staff from the personnel department or your potential manager? Will you face a panel or just one interviewer? Will there be a second round for short-listed applicants, and if so what will this involve? If necessary, phone your contact and ask.

You should also check that you know enough about the company to anticipate possible lines of questioning. As well as investigating their operations and culture, try to find out the key challenges and competition they face. Then think about how *you* can make a meaningful contribution to their efforts. Although your research should be more detailed at this stage, possible sources of information will be as before, including:

- company reports
- websites
- directories
- marketing material
- network contacts
- newspaper finance pages
- job and other advertisements

Just as the interviewer will be trying to find out what makes you tick, think about what motivates the organization. Look for key phrases in their publications or application packs, then see how you match up. The idea is not to repeat their text parrot fashion, but to spice up your delivery by introducing a little of their own terminology at key points.

Once again, go through your skills inventory, matching your

abilities to the position. Imagine yourself actually doing the job. How would you go about it? What would your unique contribution be? This may seem tedious and repetitious, but it is the best way to develop an empathy with your potential employer, making it far easier to establish a rapport on the day of the interview. As anyone in the performing arts will tell you, it takes a lot of hard work and self-discipline to come across effortlessly.

Interview Questions

No one can ever anticipate exactly what will be asked at an interview, but commonsense dictates that the main thrust will revolve around two things:

Can you do the job?
How will you fit in?

If the interviewers are from the personnel or human resources department, they will probably focus on your personal qualities, looking to screen out anyone who displays inconsistencies or does not fit into the organization's culture. In a small company, or in the second interview with a larger organization, you will probably encounter staff who have a more direct interest in your ability to do the job in hand. They will also be trying to assess how well you will get along with potential colleagues.

Whatever you are asked, keep your responses brief and concise, no more than two to three minutes. So many candidates talk for far too long, often because they are nervous or out of practice. Remember, this is a marketing exercise, and your audience will switch off rapidly if you don't get your message across smoothly and concisely.

To put this to the test, let's look at a question that comes up time and time again, usually early on in the interview: '*Tell me about yourself.*' Could you give a two-minute response? Like most people, you are probably wondering where to start. Do they want to know about your work experience, your interests or your special achievements? In fact, this is very much an ice-breaking ploy, for you and the interviewers. It gives you a unique chance to sell relevant abilities and experience on your own terms, whilst allowing them to size up your communication skills.

Whether or not the question comes up in exactly this form, preparing some bullet points in advance will help to focus your mind on the key message you want to get across in responding to this or any similar enquiry. Write them on a card, then commit them to memory. If you prefer, use a diagram or computer graphics.

Here are some more questions that come up frequently in interviews:

Q. Why do you want to work here?

A. **Use your research to show why you are keen to join the organization.**

Q. What is your greatest achievement/strength?

A. **By now you should have no trouble answering this, but tailor your response.**

Q. What is your greatest weakness/how would an enemy describe you?

A. **You have several options here, but never admit to any serious problems. Give a bland example like 'work too hard at times', or show how you *overcame* a small imperfection. One graduate scored a hit by admitting an enemy would describe him as 'too competitive', an answer neatly gauged to appeal to a fiercely competitive employer. He got the job.**

Q. Why are you better than the other candidates?

A. **A variation on 'Tell me about yourself'. Convey the same message, but use different words.**

Q. Where do you see yourself in 3 years?

A. **Again, research is the key. Know what you want within the bounds of what the organization can offer. Show you are** not solely motivated by self-interest by reiterating your interest in the *current* position.

Q. What salary are you looking for?

A. Your research should tell you the broad bands on offer elsewhere. Explain this, and say you will leave it to them to decide what your skills and experience merit. Try to avoid negotiating during the interview; leave this until they offer you the job, when you will be in a stronger bargaining position. Take other benefits into account when making your final decision.

Q. Why are you leaving your current job?

A. To advance your career. Alternatively, if you are 'downshifting', to find work that suits your new lifestyle. If you have been dismissed for whatever reason, explain the facts, without dwelling on personalities. Show how you learned from the experience. Never criticize your previous boss. Look for the positive aspects of any dubious situation.

Q. What do you think of . . . international crisis/tragedy/ scandal etc?

A. Show your knowledge of current affairs, but be careful to give a balanced view and avoid taking sides.

Q. What do you do in your spare time/to have fun?

A. Another way of sizing up your personality and motivation. Let them know you have a life outside work, but don't go overboard.

Whatever the questions, seek to bring your responses alive by painting pictures and giving examples. Be prepared to have your reactions tested with more difficult probing, such as, 'How would you solve X problem for the company?' Your pre-interview investigations may give you a clue as to the answer, but if you find yourself well and truly stumped, ask the interviewer to elaborate or give you more information. With luck you will draw the recruiters into a lively discussion, and score marks for creativity and enthusiasm.

Another tactic is to play for time by pausing before you answer. Fill any uncomfortable silence by saying something like, 'That's an interesting point . . .' Far from counting against you, this will show you as someone who is reflective and balanced. If you don't understand something, ask for clarification, and don't be afraid to ask the interviewers if they would like you to elaborate on any particular subject. Some recruiters will test your mettle by deliberately putting you under pressure, so demonstrating that you are at ease with yourself and the world is every bit as important as the content of your responses.

Make sure you have a copy of your CV or application with you; most interviewers will want you to elaborate on certain details. This is also the moment of truth if you have drawn a veil over gaps in employment. Be ready to explain how you used any periods of unemployment to your advantage, and explain what skills and experience you acquired in the process. If you are using voluntary work as an example, give it the same value you would accord to a paid job. Never diminish its worth by using terms like 'only voluntary'. Work is work, and people will treat it with the same respect that you do. The same goes for temporary jobs. Likewise, always aim to be 100 per cent positive; leave it to the interviewers to draw out any potential problems.

Some employers are totally committed to equality of opportunity, and have stringent controls in place to ensure that prejudice does not enter the equation. Others are less knowledgeable or committed, so you may well face the occasional discriminatory question. In the next chapter we will look at strategies to handle concerns about your ability to do the job, but where you face outright bigotry it may be necessary to deal with the issue head-on. You will have to decide on your own course of action, but surely it's better to tackle inappropriate behaviour, even at the risk of losing the job, than to find yourself working in an organization where such attitudes are allowed? Obviously, aim to be assertive rather than aggressive, and never be abusive or argumentative. Challenge the *facts*, not the person or their motivation.

At the end of the session, you will almost certainly be offered the chance to ask your own questions. Seize this as yet another opportunity to show enthusiasm by preparing a brief list in advance. Avoid grilling the interviewers about holidays and pay if this has not already been covered; these are subjects that can be discussed once you are offered the job. Instead, show how employer-focused and knowledgeable you are by posing questions they will enjoy answering. Tailor them to suit your own application, but some that have worked in the past include:

- I see the company is planning to expand – how will this impact your department?
- Your training and development programmes look impressive – what sessions do new recruits attend in their first year?
- How long have you been in this location?
- How many people do you employ?
- Who would I be working with?

Obviously, none of the above is meant to be copied verbatim. You will have to make up your own mind about the appropriateness of questions and responses. Indeed, in my experience, candidates often come up with outstandingly successful ideas that owe nothing to outside recommendations. By contrast, others find books on possible questions and answers extremely helpful, so get along to the library or a bookshop if you would like to read up on the subject. And, of course, the Internet is also a rich source of helpful interactive guidance, some of it highly amusing.

Rehearsing

Have a Mock Interview

If you are on a company or government programme, your adviser will probably offer a mock interview as part of the course. This can make a big difference to how you perform on the day, so make the most of the feedback and take the opportunity to time your answers. As well as comments on the quality of your responses, ask for observations on your body language and general demeanour. You may even be able to have the interview videoed, although some people find this makes them more tense than ever.

Alternatively, ask a friend or professional associate to do a practice session with you. If necessary, prepare the questions yourself, but try to find someone who has experience of interviewing, or at least knows how to give constructive feedback. A balanced appraisal will include a mix of positive observations and suggested areas for improvement. Simply pointing out your 'faults' can do more harm than good.

However, having conducted a number of real and mock interviews, I am well aware that candidates can sometimes rehearse too rigidly, with the result that they come across like amateur actors reading from an autocue. Avoid this by concentrating on the essential messages, rather than preparing word-for-word responses. This makes for a more relaxed interchange, and creates the impression that you are engaging in a spontaneous conversation. Since you can never know the precise form the questions will take, it also gives you room to think on your feet.

Do a Reconnaissance Trip

If you are not familiar with the location, a reconnaissance trip represents a very good investment in terms of checking out the journey time and getting a feel for the place. Parking facilities or train and bus journeys may look great on paper, but the reality can be an entirely different matter. After putting in so much effort why let yourself down at the last minute by turning up late? A dry run also allows you to do a little people-watching and crack the dress code. On the whole, a business suit is considered the safest option for men and women, although in the more creative fields casual wear may be the order of the day.

Do a Positive Visualization Exercise

Many people find it useful to visualize a successful outcome. After all, if you have been careful to choose a job that matches your skills, all you need now is confidence. The exercise will also help to banish any last minute self-doubts. For the best results, wait until you have done a reconnaissance trip so that you will be able to conjure up some realistic pictures. First, imagine yourself arriving at the building, feeling fresh and confident. Then visualize the interview itself, but don't bog yourself down with details. Just focus on your how good you feel as you converse with ease and make a positive impression on all concerned. It may take a few attempts, but after a while the images should start to arrive on their own, especially if you are in a relaxed frame of mind.

Focus on the Interviewers

You can also take a lot of pressure off yourself by giving some forethought to the interviewers' situation. Making choices can be a risky business, and they have a lot to lose if they get it wrong. Make an effort to see the process from their perspective, and focus on getting ready to help *them*. Although this is a very simple tension-busting technique, it can dramatically improve your performance. Anxiety comes from self-absorption, but removing our ego from the equation permits our essential vitality to shine through.

Be aware, too, that not all interviewers are trained to do the job. A real professional will know how to draw out your abilities and rephrase questions where necessary, but others may be nervous, ill-prepared, or even aggressive. Always stay calm and use your personal skills to steer the discussion in the right direction. Even with a skilled interviewer, a large part of the fun is in finding subtle ways to introduce your unique selling points, whatever the official line of questioning.

New Clothes

Where appearance is concerned, it stands to reason that you should be clean and well-groomed, but be careful about any new clothes you buy for the occasion. Dress to suit the culture of your intended employer, but give anything new at least one outing before you commit to wearing it at the interview. One young hopeful learned this to his cost, when he turned up at a recruitment evening wearing a brand-new pair of shoes. They pinched and squeezed to the point where he could think about nothing else, least of all giving intelligent answers to a somewhat bemused recruiter.

On the Day

Before the Interview

It's perfectly natural to feel nervous, and don't worry if you are too wired up to use a mind-body technique to calm yourself down. In these circumstances, the adrenaline that comes with stress may be the very thing you need to give your performance an edge. Tell yourself that once you start talking, your anxiety will disappear and everything will go smoothly from then on.

Before setting off, check that you have everything you need:

➡ comb and other grooming necessities
➡ pen, paper, diary, CV or application form
➡ *relevant* examples of achievements – keep short
➡ invitation to interview plus directions to location
➡ a note of the company's phone number – you may get held up
➡ list of referees

If you take a mobile phone, switch it off before you go in. The same goes for any other gadget that rings, pings or dings; electronic interruptions are disrespectful and decidedly uncool.

On Arrival

Plan to arrive 15 minutes early, which will allow you use the facilities and generally settle in. Get yourself into the right mood by smiling and greeting reception staff politely. They can be very important allies, particularly in small companies, where they may well be asked to contribute an opinion of you. A little pre-interview sociability can also help to loosen you up for the challenge ahead. This struck home forcefully when I accompanied a deaf candidate to a successful interview. While waiting to see the director, we took the opportunity to chat to a very hospitable receptionist, who was also the switchboard operator. Not only did it prove a very effective warm-up exercise, but I had no trouble at all in getting through to the director when I made the follow-up call.

During the Interview

It takes a matter of seconds for someone to form a first impression of you, so make every moment count. When you greet the interviewer (or interviewers), smile, look them in the eye and shake hands firmly. If they offer you a cup of coffee, I would suggest you politely decline the invitation. It's unlikely that you'll get much chance to drink it anyway, and there's always the possibility of a spillage. Taking a few deep breaths will help to dispel any nerves, and take courage from the fact that you will not look anything like as anxious as you feel. Remember: *as soon as you start talking, your nerves will disappear*.

Your body language and mannerisms will also be under the spotlight, so:

➡ Seat yourself in a comfortable position, changing the angle of the chair if necessary.
➡ Sit up, and keep your hands in your lap.
➡ Don't wave your arms about or make exaggerated gestures.
➡ Concentrate on good posture and a clear and confident vocal delivery.
➡ If you want to cross your legs, do a 'low-cross' at the ankle – this looks less defensive.
➡ Continue to take deep breaths if you feel anxious.
➡ Slow down a little if nerves are getting the better of you.
➡ Look enthusiastic, and smile from time to time.
➡ Show you are listening by leaning forward and nodding at appropriate points.
➡ Maintain comfortable eye contact, but don't stare.
➡ If you are addressing a panel, give each interviewer equal attention as you answer questions.
➡ Be sensitive in your use of humour. What's funny to you may be offensive to someone else.

As you can see, there is a lot to think about, which is why it is so important to have a practice session and get feedback beforehand. Obviously, if relaxation techniques are a regular part of your life, your reactions will be far more spontaneous and you will be less likely to tense up. This is equally true of people who make a habit of using assertive behaviour. Despite this, I am often faced with the objection, 'But I won't be myself.' In fact, this is not true. You are not being encouraged to change your personality, but simply to use a few tried and tested professional techniques to boost your performance.

Like any good performer, make sure you end on a strong note. Whether the session has gone well or otherwise, smile and thank the interviewer(s) for their time. As soon as you get home, write a short thank-you letter and reiterate your interest in the position. Small courtesies like this can give you a big edge on your rivals. Finally, make a note of everything you can recall about the interview while it's still fresh in your mind. This will help you to analyse your performance and prepare for any further rounds in the process.

Next Steps

There are now several things that can happen:

- you get the job
- you are turned down
- you are put 'on file'
- you hear nothing
- you are called to a further interview

Let's look at these one by one.

You Get the Job

Naturally you will be delighted, but pause for reflection before rushing to accept. Is there anything to negotiate first, like salary or other benefits? You are now in a strong bargaining position, so go for it. Alternatively, now that you've seen the organization at close range, do you still want the job? If you find it difficult to decide, write down the pros and cons on a piece of paper and discuss it with someone else. Is there anything you need to clarify?

Whatever your final decision, send a written response and be *positive*. Clearly, if you are accepting you need only say 'thank you' and explain how much you are looking forward to starting. If you are turning them down, think up an acceptable reason for doing so but tell them how much you valued their time and so on. 'Owing to unforeseen circumstances' is a good excuse. Just because an employer is not to your taste at this stage doesn't mean you might not want to reapply if circumstances change. Always aim to exit nicely, and leave the door ajar. Who knows, in these days of merger mania you might end up working for them anyway.

You are Turned Down

Being turned down is never easy for anyone, but stewing about it only makes matters worse. Lorna was distraught on getting two rejection letters in the same week. However, she rallied quickly, and decided that although she would prepare just as carefully, she would treat all future interviews as rehearsals. In fact, there was only one more, and this time she made the grade. Lorna had no doubt that her new philosophy was at the heart of her success. 'It was as if my "luck" changed overnight, and all my anxiety disappeared.'

In another case, after a string of rejections, a candidate found himself on the verge of giving up. Up to that point he had been reluctant to ask for feedback but this time he relented. It turned out that he had all the right qualities but was lacking in a specific area of experience. He remedied this by taking on some voluntary work, and eventually found the position he wanted. Of course, it's not always this easy and some employers will refuse to give any meaningful comments. The point is you will never know until you try. I can certainly report a significant success rate among the candidates I have helped.

And, of course, no matter how bad you feel, if you are still interested in the organization send a thank-you letter, and try to leave the door open for a future approach. You could use something along the lines of 'Congratulations on filling the position successfully. I very much enjoyed meeting you and am still very interested in working for xxxx. Perhaps you could keep my application on file in case any suitable vacancies arise in the future?'

In true campaign spirit, you will then press on with other applications. Never put all your hopes into one job, no matter how perfect it seems. Nothing is worse then hanging around day after day, biting your nails and praying for that one special letter to land on your mat.

You are 'Put on File'

Obviously, by now you know exactly what to do. Say 'thank you' and reaffirm your interest.

You Hear Nothing

Follow up – smile and dial.

You are called to a Further Interview

If you are short-listed for a second interview, congratulate yourself, but don't neglect to get some more practice. Use your notes to prepare another rehearsal session.

Other Selection Methods

As well as the interview, you may well face other tests and assessments, most of which are designed to screen out unsuitable candidates. In days gone by, these methods were largely confined to executive or graduate recruitment, but in recent times they are being used more extensively. They may consist of a single test or a series of exercises and group activities held at an assessment centre over a day or more. Tests are also increasingly likely to be presented on computer, where you will be asked to type in a response or asked to press a particular key to indicate your choice of answers.

Here are some of the battery of techniques used:

Psychometric Tests

Used to assess personality traits and problem-solving abilities, the very thought of these tests can strike fear into the heart of even the most capable candidate. Despite growing disquiet about possible unfairness to women and ethnic groups, they are still popular with many employers. A new, allegedly fairer range of assessments is currently under scrutiny, but it can take years for advances to find their way into mainstream use.

You may not be able to change the system, but there are several things you can do to ease the pain. No matter how tempting it may be to present what you think is the desired profile, psychologists advise that the best policy is to answer personality questions honestly. In any case, most questionnaires have built-in safeguards to detect where people are trying to distort the results. Give your brain a good workout beforehand by getting hold of some books on the subject and/or accessing some of the many self-assessment sites on the Internet. If testers are willing to send you some sample questionnaires in advance, so much the better. On the day, read the instructions carefully, and make the most of any pre-test practice session. This is also the time to raise any queries.

Most ability tests get progressively more difficult, so pace yourself accordingly. The questions are designed to stretch even the brightest people, so don't worry if you can't answer them all. The issue is not how clever you are, but if and how you will fit into the role/environment, which is why even the most gifted candidates can score poorly. Anyway, why would you want to take a job for which you are not really suited? Even if you are unsuccessful think positively and try to get some feedback, at least verbally. You may even get a full written report, something that would cost you dear if you went to an independent consultant.

Basic Aptitude Tests

Often used in the recruitment of administrative and secretarial staff, these are designed to test a range of abilities, from spelling and arithmetic to typing speed and office systems knowledge. You may also be asked to fill in missing letters or words or to complete a sequence of numbers.

Presentations

Here you will be asked to give a presentation on a particular subject, usually within a set time limit. You should be given advance notice of facilities and materials, but if in doubt ask. The most common medium is the overhead projector, but you might also be expected to use a flip chart or board. Rehearse your pitch thoroughly, preferably in front of someone who is able to give constructive feedback.

Observed Group Activities

These take a variety of forms, but essentially the observers are looking to see what role you adopt in the group, and how you relate to the other members. It may involve a discussion or debate, a problem-solving exercise or role playing. How well you do will depend on your level of self-awareness and your understanding of exactly what the job requires. Go through the job description and make your own assessment of what the observers will be looking for. For instance, if you are going for a management job, leadership skills will feature high on the list.

Whatever the position in question, seemingly small things can earn important points. Demonstrating an awareness of others' needs will always count in your favour, as will picking up the pen and offering to be the scribe. There are many different ways to show initiative, and pushy types do not necessarily come out best.

In-tray Exercise

Candidates are asked to tackle a series of tasks, from prioritizing paperwork to drafting letters. It can involve any aspect of the job you are applying for, so do your homework.

Doing the Job

This involves going into the workplace for a hands-on attempt at doing the job. The time allotted can be anything from a few hours to a whole day. Again, the more you know about the organization and the position, the easier it will be to anticipate the duties.

Telephone Screening

Sometimes used in the initial stages of recruitment for jobs involving a lot of telephone work. If possible, practise with an adviser or friend in advance. Use the techniques described in the last chapter to boost your performance. Remember, the 'interviewer' is unable to look for non-verbal clues, so use your voice to maximum effect.

Video Link-ups

'Virtual' screening looks set to grow, particularly where companies recruit from overseas. Faced with a video link-up, practise first with a camcorder to get used to seeing yourself on screen. You will only be seen from the waist up, so keep your hands out of the way and concentrate on your voice and facial expressions.

Lunch

The idea is to put you at ease, but the lunch interview can also engender a false sense of security, so watch the alcohol consumption and don't get too familiar. Whether you are in the running for an internal promotion or being head-hunted from the outside, make sure you prepare in advance.

Graphology

Puts your handwriting under the scrutiny of experts to detect personality traits. Not much you can do about this, but the feedback should be interesting (assuming you know what's going on).

SUMMARY

* Ease the pain of interviews by seeing them as a discussion and empathizing with the interviewers.

* Try to anticipate lines of questioning by fine-tuning your knowledge of the employer.
* Get into the swing by having at least one practice interview and doing a reconnaissance trip.
* Dress to suit the culture of the organization and use positive body language.
* Find out if you have to undergo tests or other assessments and prepare accordingly.

Chapter Twelve

Adapting Your Strategy

Background and status can have a significant effect on how the employer views the cost of employing you, including the amount of time it will take to integrate you into the organization.

How you manage your career and approach your job search is very much a matter of personal choice, and no book can cover all the angles. However, your situation in life will certainly have a bearing on how you go about your task, and it will often influence how employers view your abilities. It can also have a dramatic effect on how well you perform once you have found the work you want.

Perception is not something that can be captured and put under a microscope, but over the years I have detected common themes affecting certain 'communities', particularly:

➡ graduates and other young people
➡ 'older' candidates and executives
➡ long-term unemployed people
➡ women returning to the job market
➡ people with disabilities

Grouping individuals in this way is merely a convenient device to customize guidance for people who may face common challenges, so don't be put off by the terminology. For example, in career terms, 'older' is often used to describe people as young as forty, an age when most workers have just reached their peak. In fact, executives can be put out to pasture at the tender age of thirty-five.

Likewise, 'disabled' has no fixed meaning. Depending on your point of view, it can be the impairment itself or the disabling attitudes it engenders in others.

You may fall into several categories at once or be part of another community. For instance, in previous chapters we looked at dealing with outright prejudice, which affects a far wider range of candidates, including ethnic minorities, gay men and lesbians. Here, however, we are not concerned with blatant discrimination, but with perceived strengths and weaknesses in relation to *how you match up to the job* and the *cost* to the employer. Cost will be measured not only in financial terms, but also in the light of how much time and effort it will take to integrate you into the organization.

Whether or not you are included in the above descriptions, read through all the sections. In taking the time to appreciate the challenges faced by others, you will be considerably enhancing your repertoire of interpersonal skills, while also gaining a valuable insight into the competition you face. Not only that, your circumstances will no doubt change with the passing of time, so it makes good sense to think ahead. Make sure, too, that you do the exercise at the end of the chapter.

Graduates and Other Young People

On the positive side, young people are seen as:

- quick to learn
- open to new ideas
- enthusiastic
- energetic
- fit and healthy
- on top of new technology

If you have done well in your studies, whether at university, college or school, you can additionally credit yourself with being highly competent and well-organized. You should also be accustomed to making optimum use of the library and computerized resources, which gives you a huge advantage when it comes to managing your own career. The Internet, for example, is bursting with sites designed to help young people along the professional path.

On the minus side, many younger candidates suffer from lack of:

⇒ work experience
⇒ self-reliance skills
⇒ realistic expectations
⇒ patience
⇒ political awareness

Although employers are queuing up to get the 'best' graduates, and offering rich rewards in return, remember that a degree in itself is no longer a passport to success. Today's organizations expect the best of all possible worlds, and you should also be prepared to demonstrate initiative and strong interpersonal skills, preferably gained through work.

Paul's story illustrates just how important commercial exposure can be, even where an academic high achiever is concerned. After leaving school, he spent a year in my team at IBM before going on to gain a good degree at Oxford. He also took a variety of summer jobs, both in the UK and overseas. Paul has no doubt that this diversity of experience played a key role in helping him to beat off fierce competition from other graduates for a position with a leading consultancy firm.

At the other end of the spectrum, Beth left school with few qualifications and no work experience. When her solo attempts to find paid employment failed, she used her initiative to gain a place on a state-sponsored youth training scheme, including a short-term placement with an employer. This not only revealed a previously untapped aptitude for office systems, but also allowed her to build up other practical and social skills. At the end of the scheme, she took several temporary jobs, eventually finding a permanent position as an administrator.

For those of you who are not graduates, bear in mind that

there are armies of successful people out there who have never been through college or university, including many entrepreneurs. Anyone with talent and drive can make out in the new world of work, no matter how lacking in formal education they may be. Qualifications can be acquired at any stage in your life, but nothing can compensate for lack of creativity and initiative.

Where self-reliance is concerned, having trained and supervised hundreds of young people, I would recommend that you make every effort to cultivate your powers of initiative. This goes hand in hand with being realistic about what to expect in your first job. The workplace can be very different from school or university. Multi-tasking and tight deadlines can come as a huge culture shock, and no matter how well-intentioned the organization, you will often have to create your own opportunities. Periods of hyperactivity may be followed by days of having nothing to do, and help from pressurized managers and colleagues is not always easy to find.

Once again, the solution is to think about other people as well as yourself. For a busy boss or mentor, constantly having to find 'interesting' tasks for a new recruit can be very wearing. No job provides constant stimulation, and there are always boring duties to be taken care of. If you can accept this, and get stuck into the dull stuff as well as the more attractive assignments, you will be a long way down the road to self-reliance.

Taking a mature and patient approach in the early days can also be used as a ploy to negotiate a better deal for yourself later on. For instance, if you feel that you are being neglected, explain that you are doing your share of the routine work, but ask if this can be balanced with more demanding projects. If you want early responsibility, you could also lighten your manager's load by writing your own objectives.

At all costs, steer clear of Willie Whinge and Gabbie Gossip. Outsiders, and losers by their own hand, these types often attach themselves to young recruits as self-appointed mentors. Treat what you hear with caution, and be sparing in offering your opinions. Have the courage of your convictions, and don't be disillusioned by any political manoeuvring. This is all part of every-day working life, and you will soon develop the assertiveness to deal with it your own way.

For those who do possess the winning combination of practical skills and drive, opportunities abound. Industries where young professionals excel, often making a fortune in the process, include:

⇒ computing
⇒ communications
⇒ finance
⇒ fashion
⇒ entertainment and the media
⇒ sport
⇒ publishing
⇒ advertising

'Older' Candidates and Executives

As an experienced professional your greatest strength is maturity, something you can exploit to the full in an interview. Maturity suggests that you have:

⇒ a proven work record
⇒ strong social skills
⇒ a self-reliant attitude
⇒ patience

However, you may also encounter some of the myths surrounding the older worker, namely that you lack:

⇒ energy
⇒ receptivity to new ideas
⇒ good health
⇒ competence with new technology

These perceptions are less likely when you are moving from one job to another, but they take on greater significance when you are out of work.

Health and energy are important for everyone, but once we reach our middle years, it usually requires a little more work. As we saw in Chapter Three, one of the best ways to demonstrate continued vigour is to include some form of active pastime in your leisure interests. Even a daily run or swim will look good on your CV, and the benefits will no doubt be reflected in your general appearance.

Mind-body techniques can also bring a substantial pay-off as we grow older, as research into the effects of transcendental meditation demonstrates. In one study, a group of people with an average age of fifty, who had been practising the technique for five or more years, were compared to matched controls using the Adult Growth Examination (a test measuring indicators of biological age: systolic blood pressure, hearing and eyesight). The findings were that the biological age of long-term users of the technique was, on average, twelve years less than their actual chronological age. Food for thought indeed!

Any objections on the grounds that you are set in your ways, and will find it difficult to take on new ideas, can be handled by giving examples to prove otherwise. If necessary, devote some extra time to recalling and listing the key projects that have stretched your creative powers to profitable effect. All employers are motivated by profit, whether in the form of money or other ambitions, so light up their lives with a little good news about what you have delivered in the past and can project for the future.

The only way to dispel fears about your grasp of technology is to get on top of it. This doesn't necessarily mean becoming a technical wizard, but if you have managed to survive without learning the most popular office applications, book on a course right now. A reasonable knowledge of the Internet will also work to your advantage.

The other big issue for executives/senior personnel is salary expectations. Organizations may well be tempted to give preference to younger, less expensive staff, so if you are finding it difficult to get the job you want, it could be worth weighing up whether you can afford to take a drop in income. A little soul-searching might also be in order. Ask yourself: 'Do I need the money, or is it a matter of pride?' By all means go for the best, but is it worth holding yourself back just to maintain such a questionable mark of esteem?

On the other hand, think hard before you choose to get out of the rat race by taking the radical option of downshifting. Trading a good income for a better quality of life may sound attractive, but do your sums first. Following your heart is all very well, but not if it means living on the breadline.

We have already looked at the option of consultancy work, but another viable alternative for the executive is interim management. This involves offering yourself for short-term assignments to solve specific problems or holding the fort in the absence of other executives. Since the work may well be patchy, it is probably better suited to those of you who are cushioned with a redundancy payment or occupational pension.

As for the best approach to job search, anyone who has reached a position of seniority should certainly put networking at the top of their list. For you, access to the hidden job market is absolutely essential. Executive recruitment consultancies will no doubt do their best for you, but they will also be able to pick and choose from an impressive candidate list. By all means sign up with them, but keep in regular touch with your own contacts, and stay alert for opportunities to approach organizations directly.

Senior or otherwise, you might also want to ask yourself if you can afford to take time out to get a first, or additional, professional or academic qualification. These days, more people than ever are returning to university as mature students, and there is no longer any convincing argument for being 'too old to learn'. If people in their seventies and eighties can do it, there's certainly no reason why someone in mid-life should feel embarrassed about going to college.

Perhaps the most encouraging news for 'third age' candidates comes from California, where the LifePlan Centre in San Francisco helps the over-fifties to take a new direction personally and professionally, with an emphasis on the holistic approach. Here people can attend training courses, use mentoring services and access information resources, all for a very modest fee. It is to be hoped that programmes like this will eventually find their way into mainstream career development initiatives around the world.

Long-term Unemployed People

Being out of work for an extended period is a painful and soul-destroying experience. Or is it? How would you react to the idea that losing your job represents *an opportunity for growth on an unprecedented scale*? With disbelief at the insensitivity and callousness of such a suggestion? This is only to be expected, because for most people being unemployed for any significant length of time brings on feelings of rejection and isolation, which if left unchecked can all too easily lead to the 3D reaction:

➡ Disappointment
➡ Demotivation
➡ Depression

But, fortunately, it doesn't have to be this way. For you, just as for everybody else, success depends on drawing up a customized campaign, and sticking to it. This is not to minimize the very real challenges you may face, but to assert the equally real power you have over your own future.

First and foremost you are not unemployed. You may not be in *paid* employment, but that is a different matter. Think about it: what does 'employed' mean? In essence, it means nothing more than being 'occupied or busy', and anyone engaged in active job searching certainly fulfils both criteria. Obviously, if you can also be doing something that resembles a paid job, so much the better.

So where is the opportunity in all this? Well, unlike most people, your temporary withdrawal from the rat race means that, like it or not, you have more *time* at your disposal. Time to look at yourself and your aspirations; time to practise relaxation techniques and think about acquiring new skills; time to plan and execute a vigorous job search or career development plan. Of course, money problems can take their toll, but these are likely to be even worse if you don't take the opportunity to overhaul your strategy. You are now in a position to make one of the best investments of your life, but it will take dedication and self-discipline.

Your campaign plan will be essentially the same as for other job seekers, but be sure to:

➡ Establish a **regular routine**. This is often the first thing to go when there are no external demands on your time. Try to get up and go to bed at the same time each 'working' day. Get yourself into the right frame of mind by dressing in the clothes you would normally wear to work, and pay exactly the same attention to grooming. If you look professional, you will feel professional.

➡ Engage in the supremely important art of **networking**. Don't be disheartened if old 'friends' and contacts drop off. This is a very common experience, and a sign that you need an injection of fresh blood. If one door closes, knock on another one. You know how it's done, so get out there and do it.

➡ Capitalize on any **free** help you can get. Government programmes may not sound very glamorous, but they can bring rewards if you take a proactive approach. I know of endless cases where a state scheme has catapulted people into a whole new life. In one instance, an unskilled candidate, who had not worked for four years, found himself on a fast-track to management within three months of finding a job in this way.

➡ **Divest yourself** of any extra responsibilities that have crept into your routine simply because other people think you have nothing else to do. There is a big difference between helping out here and there and filling your whole life with duties that prevent you from pursuing your own goals. However, be sensitive about how and when you extricate yourself. If necessary, do it by degrees, especially if members of the family are involved.

This is also an ideal time to think about developing a unique selling point. Smooth operators in the commercial world are always on the lookout for chances to make themselves indispensable, so why not you? One inspiring example was a technophobic woman who decided to take her fears in hand by spending three hours a day finding her way round a variety of computer packages. It was a long, hard slog, but her technical competence made all the difference when it came to getting a job in finance.

Women Returning to the Job Market

The good news for you is that one in three workers in a woman with a family, and more and more are moving into management and executive positions. This hasn't escaped the attention of employers, who are beginning to realize that family-friendly policies, including flexible working hours, make good business sense.

There is also a rapid growth in women taking the entrepreneurial path by setting up their own businesses, which they often run from home. In fact these days many a lucrative deal is clinched from the spare room. Why waste money on expensive premises when you can just as easily keep in touch with staff or consultants via e-mail or tele-conferencing facilities?

At another level, the stereotypical view of the secretary as typist and tea-maker is being consigned to the history books. These days women are far more likely to see the role as a springboard to the executive suite. This is hardly surprising, given the diversity of interpersonal, technical and organizational abilities required of the profession. No problem there in making yourself indispensable (and learning all about the business in the process).

So this is the new world of opportunity, and the outlook for women is good. But exactly how are you to go about staging a successful comeback? Returning to a radically transformed labour market can clearly present a range of obstacles, especially if you have been off the scene for a long time, perhaps waiting for the children to fly the nest before making your move. On the other hand, if your children are still young, you may have to grapple with the problems of finding adequate child care and juggling home responsibilities with work.

Let's start by looking at the situation from the recruiters' perspective. Their main fear will be that your skills and experience are out-of-date, and in many cases this will be true. The only solution is to take an honest look at your abilities, and decide if you are ready for a job, or whether you need to undertake some preparatory training. If you decide on the latter, it may help to go back to Chapter Eight and weigh up the different options for training and getting work experience. Check too with adult education centres who often run courses aimed at women returners, sometimes incorporating tuition in the English language for people from overseas.

There is no easy solution to the child care challenge, and this is one you will have to work out for yourself. Finding an employer with crèche facilities is no simple task, but you may strike lucky. However, it's more likely that you will have to budget for care, unless there is someone in the family willing to help out. Even if you plan to work from home, it might be a good idea to check if you can afford some domestic help. No matter how advanced their organizational skills, mothers tend to put their own needs last, so taking time out for relaxation will take skilful advanced planning.

If school holidays are your problem, try asking employers if they would be willing to offer you work on a 'term-time only' basis. Banks and supermarkets may be your best bet, but there is nothing to stop you approaching other organizations, especially if they have a culture of flexible working methods.

If your contact list has dwindled over the years, now comes the time to start building it up again. Women are natural networkers, and you should make every effort to join a professional association where you can meet as many people as possible. Go to any professional event and you will see just how large the female contingent of high flyers has become. Obviously, if the demands on your time are already heavy, formal functions may have to wait a while, but don't leave it too long. Getting back into circulation can be demanding at first, but it will pay huge dividends in the long run.

Of course, it would be unrealistic to say that all women are enjoying rewarding careers. Many are trapped in low-paid, unskilled jobs, from which it can take a great deal of effort to escape. If you need a quick injection of cash, and find that you have to settle for such work, see it as a short-term solution and don't lose sight of your longer-term goals.

On the subject of finances, making up for loss of retirement income is yet another consideration for the woman returner, and one that is easily overlooked when there are so many more immediate problems vying for your attention. However, if you find a new employer with an occupational pension scheme, it would certainly be worth asking about making additional voluntary contributions to boost the value of your annuity. The alternative is to shop around for the best private arrangement you can find. If all this seems too much at the moment, add it to your list of things to think about in the not-too-distant future.

The other great barrier for many returners is lack of confidence, but don't let that hold you back. In my experience, more and more bosses are waking up to the fact that mothers, with their well-advanced interpersonal skills and talent for multi-tasking, represent outstanding value for money. Take the case of the manager who employed a secretary who could not type and had not worked for five years. What was the reason for such seeming madness? A very straightforward one; he realized that her down-to-earth approach, plus a proven ability to learn quickly, were worth all the technical experience offered by competing candidates. Commonsense and self-reliance may sound mundane, but they are qualities that will never go out of fashion in the world of work.

People with Disabilities

Having a disability does not in itself mean you will have difficulty finding work or advancing your career. However, I have worked in partnership with a significant number of disabled candidates to overcome the problems that do exist, and it is this experience I would like to share.

In the past, disability issues were rarely part of mainstream education or employer consciousness, but fortunately times are changing. Slowly but surely myths are being dispelled and measures are being put in place to ensure equality of access for all. However, there is still a long way to go, and many disabled people are still being deprived of employment opportunities. This is not only sad for the people concerned, but for employers, who are missing out on large reserves of talent.

In my view, the main barriers to employment are:

➧ fear of the unknown amongst employers
➧ widespread ignorance about the relatively simple adjustments to working methods and equipment required by certain individuals

Dispelling fear is largely a matter of using effective communication skills to explain and discuss the facts around any particular disability. You may be able to do this on your own, or it may entail getting someone else to help you. Let me give you some examples of how others have gone about it:

When a deaf candidate found work with a local organization, I organized two deaf awareness workshops, during which she gave a demonstration of sign language. Management staff were totally committed to the initiative, and ensured that the entire workforce attended, including the chief executive. The sessions proved remarkably effective in facilitating future communications, and many of the staff realized for the first time that deaf people have a rich linguistic culture. They also learned how to facilitate lip-reading, enjoyed a demonstration of a doorbell that activates a flashing light, and had the opportunity to use a text phone.

On finding a job involving a great deal of typing, a client with a visual disability relieved her employer's concerns by providing her own magnifying equipment. In other cases, people have persuaded the organization to finance equipment and/or support workers.

A man with epilepsy explained to recruiting staff that there was nothing to fear if he had a seizure at work, and went on to detail how those around him could help. This was followed by a video which outlined the different forms of the condition and acted out a variety of scenarios.

Naturally, the above examples only scratch the surface. There are so many types of so-called disabilities that it would be impossible to cover them all. In fact, hidden impairments, including disease and mental health needs, sometimes pose the greatest challenge of all. However, the principle of overcoming objections is always the same: focus on what you *can* do and be ready to sweep away any groundless fears entertained by the employer.

Like all other candidates, you are in the business of providing solutions and showing how you get results. If you need any help with this, check out if you are entitled to any support from state-funded schemes or voluntary organizations. Make enquiries at your local Job Centre or State Employment Office, and check the telephone directories for disability support organizations, who may also be able to help you to interpret disability discrimination legislation and identify employers who are sincerely committed to equality of opportunity.

Self-Assessment

Photocopy the chart below and use it to list your plus and minus points, bearing in mind that the influencing forces will be a mixture of those imposed by others and those arising from your own beliefs and fears. If your experience or observations are different from what you have read here, by all means follow your own wisdom. You can also find out a great deal more by talking to other people.

Keep the completed chart in your portfolio to help you prepare for interviews and any other aspects of your campaign, including getting started in a new job. Tables like this can also be used as an

Positive Factors (External)	Barriers (External)

Positive Factors (Internal)	Barriers (Internal)

Action Plan to Address Barriers:

aid in analysing any other aspect of your life. Even the most daunting projects can be tamed by the simple expedient of a graphic analysis.

SUMMARY

* Energy, enthusiasm and technical competence all work in favour of the younger candidate, but you also need self-reliance skills.
* Experience and maturity give the older candidate a significant edge, but you may need to dispel myths about lack of energy and creativity.
* Those who have been out of work for some time can become isolated and depressed, so an established routine and regular outside contact are essential.
* The outlook is good for women returners, but you must be prepared to update your skills and build up your contact list.
* If you have a disability, be prepared to tackle misconceptions and educate employers on any adjustments needed to help you do the job.

Part Three

Making
it
Happen

Chapter Thirteen

Begin It Now

Whatever you can do or dream
you can, begin it.
Boldness has genius, power and
magic in it.
Begin it now.

GOETHE

Review

So, now, as we approach the end of the course, it's time to summarize what we have covered so far, then move on to the final stage: implementation.

Let's start by reviewing the previous chapters:

1. The real revolution in the world of work will be driven by individuals who have learned to balance the profusion of external information with the wealth of liberating knowledge within.

2. There will always be anxiety and tension in our lives, but stress itself is not the problem. The problem is how we *respond* to events. The secret of success is to take the 3Rs approach; Relax, Refresh Renew.

3. In the new millennium, fitness and health issues will be central to the workplace culture, but it makes sense to take charge of your own well-being.

4. Setting positive goals is the number one priority in getting what you want out of life. This goes hand in hand with effective time management.

5. Qualifications and professional aptitude count for little if

you do not develop political awareness at work. Become a warrior in the workplace.

6. In modern times, everyone is looking for the *feelgood* factor, and the individual who delivers this will reap the rewards, financially and emotionally. Be positive and learn to think like an entrepreneur.

7. Personal recommendations play a huge part in spreading the word about your capabilities. The wider your network, the better your chances of advancing your career and finding the work that's right for you.

8. The future belongs to candidates who develop career resilience and practise lifelong learning. Successful career management entails optimum use of organizational and interpersonal skills.

9. A CV is not a list of jobs, but a powerful piece of advertising material. The results you get will be in direct proportion to the amount of time you devote to its preparation.

10. Finding a job is a job in itself, deserving all the time and attention you would give to any other professional assignment. Mount a personal campaign plan.

11. It takes a matter of seconds for an interviewer to form a first impression of you, so make every moment count. Other forms of assessment are equally important. Meticulous preparation is the key to success.

12. Background and status can have a significant effect on how the employer views the cost of employing you, including the amount of time it will take to integrate you into the organization. Adapt your strategy accordingly.

We have come a long way together, but now comes the time for you to take charge. How are you going to set about putting what you have learned into practice? As with any new project, the planning often seems more exciting than the actual implementation phase. This is even more so when you are in the driving seat.

However, you must remember that nothing will happen until you make a firm *commitment* to bring about change. We all suffer from the temptation to put things off, but this is not a luxury you can afford in the new world of work, where survival depends on keeping your finger on the pulse, and taking *action* to ensure that you always stay on top of developments. Procrastination is simply not an option.

From now on, you should make it a top priority to keep the energy flowing. We have already looked at several ways to do this, but as is customary at the end of a training course let's revisit the fundamental principles and examine some new techniques.

Six Ways to Motivate Yourself

Be Bold

Does boldness really contain the secret of genius, power and magic? If it does, then what better quality for the Millennium Candidate to cultivate? The only way to discover the truth is to test it for yourself. But first, you will have to explore exactly what 'boldness' means. The dictionary gives a variety of definitions, chief among which are 'courage' and 'enterprise'. These, of course, are exactly the qualities we have been examining throughout the book.

It is this combination of courage and enterprise that ultimately distinguishes the winner from the loser, whatever it is you are competing for. Getting started on a new lifestyle will almost certainly entail some discomfort in the early days, but this is a valuable part of development. Certainly, we all feel anxiety, but we don't have to own it. The big question is this: 'Am I this bundle of fear, prejudices and conditioned responses that makes up my everyday experience, or do I have a more powerful and liberated self?'

If you have the boldness to ask the question, sincerely and honestly, you are already well on the way to the answer. However, this is not something to be solved on an intellectual level. The only way to know the truth is to regularly experience inner silence and harmony. This is the point at which we go beyond diversity, even psychology. Instructors and books can point the way, but to understand the reality, you must do the work yourself.

Until you locate the source of real power, any attempt to reinvent yourself will, at best, be of a superficial and temporary nature. By contrast, if you regularly bring your attention back to the 'now' by letting go of any hurt or pain in the silence of your deeper consciousness, you will emerge afresh each day, without an accumulation of limiting beliefs from the past. Once you have established this inner foundation you will be ready for more creative experimentation and adventure on the outside.

We have discussed self-marketing techniques at great length, but to be really effective they must be used with subtlety and style. We are not aiming for a 'hard sell' approach, but a natural and spontaneous interaction with potential 'buyers'. Once you achieve an inward balance, outward poise becomes much easier to attain. In combination, they add up to a potent formula for success.

Some people manage inner development perfectly well on their own, but others prefer group involvement. This is another form of networking with the difference that your confidants should be chosen with even greater care. Your deeper insights are a precious commodity, not to be shared with all and sundry. Fortunately, if you take up a mind-body technique you will almost certainly meet people of like mind in the process. Regular contact with friends and associates who share your aspirations and values is one of the best ways to stay motivated.

Hold the Vision

No matter how strong our early ambitions, as time passes our dreams are often abandoned, remaining buried under an avalanche of everyday responsibilities and worries. Once we are locked into the mundane, it is very easy to lose our sense of the extraordinary and magical. How easy it is to take the line of least resistance and settle for the humdrum existence that becomes the lot of so many, even the most talented. It is not a question of money; wealthy people are just as likely to abandon their dreams as the rest of us, all the time wondering what might have happened if they had had the courage of their original convictions.

Don't let this happen to you. For a start, photocopy the above summary, and keep it in the front of your portfolio. As already discussed, specific goals can be written down, cut out and stuck up somewhere where you will see them on a regular basis. Cards or computerized prompts can be used in a similar fashion to record inspirational quotes or reminders. At work, use posters to remind you of team objectives.

Capitalize on Colour

Colour has enormous potential to lift the spirits and help us stay motivated, a fact that has not been lost on philosophers, psychologists and therapists over the years. However, you don't have to be an expert to appreciate the positive effect it can have on our feelings and moods. Not only that, used creatively, it can transform our looks, which is why image consultants are often able to regenerate their clients' careers with a simple colour make-over.

Not everyone will relate to a particular colour in the same way, but here are some of the more popular associations:

Green is for healing and peace, which is why it is often used in hospitals or other settings where a calming influence is desirable. Of course, one of the best ways to appreciate the colour is to get out into nature and enjoy the enormous variety of shades to be found in the foliage of trees and bushes.

Blue, one of the most popular colours, is also calming and healing. Just think what a pleasure it is to look up at a clear blue sky. It might also have a pacifying effect on an adversary in a confrontational situation.

Red can be highly stimulating and energizing, but sometimes overly so, hence its association with anger and danger. If you are constantly feeling on edge, it may be that you have too much around the home.

Orange may be a safer choice when looking for an invigorating influence.

Yellow can be enormously uplifting, especially if you are suffering from lack of light in winter.

Purple symbolizes spirituality, which is why it is so often used in churches and other places of sanctuary. It can also be useful in creating the right mood for meditation.

Most of us pay at least some attention to colour when choosing clothes or the decor in our homes, although style and fashion considerations probably win out over the effect it can have on our spirits and the moods of those around us. If you have never thought seriously about these benefits, try focusing on a specific colour and examine the effect it has on you. For example:

If you need a quick injection of confidence, close your eyes and imagine an orange light diffusing through your body. Stay with it for a few seconds, then open your eyes and check out how you feel. If it has the desired effect, you can use it as a technique to energize yourself before an interview or any other ordeal.

To calm yourself down before or after a challenging event, use the same technique with the colour blue. Sky blue is usually a safe bet, but use any shade that appeals to you.

How well you do depends to a large extent on your general receptivity to colour and your overall powers of imagination. If it doesn't work for you, forget about it; straining to get a result will defeat the object. There are also certain medical conditions where imagery like this may have a harmful effect. Always check first with a doctor if you think there is even the slightest chance of a negative reaction.

Harness Energy with Feng Shui

Feng Shui, which originated in China over 4,000 years ago, is yet another example of how the West is learning from Eastern practices. Its central premise is that everything in your surroundings can contribute to the success or failure of your endeavours. Feng Shui is now being used to productive effect by individuals all over the world. It also looks set to be of interest to corporations.

Feng Shui experts believe that arranging your home or workplace to harness the benefit of positive energies can have very specific effects on your career. It can help you to find work, get promoted or achieve an all-round improvement in performance. This is one reason why more and more people are using Feng Shui consultants to advise on interior decoration. For those of you on a tighter budget, there are a variety of splendid step-by-step guides on the market.

Boost your Memory

There's no need to wait until you face a selection test to boost your cerebral skills. Taking charge of your own career means that you will have to commit a range of facts and figures to memory, so follow the lead of corporate high-flyers by improving your retentive and creative powers with regular mental exercise. Just a little practice can produce impressive results.

The latest scientific research also suggests that, in active and healthy brains, there is no loss of cells with age. In fact, the evidence points to an *increase* in intelligence, *if the brain is used and trained effectively*. You don't even have to go on a course; just get hold of a good book or do the quizzes that appear regularly in newspapers and magazines. For business use, try the technique covered in Tony Buzan's *The Mind Map Book*, which can transform your powers of analysis and presentation. It might also be helpful with exam revision.

Laugh at Yourself

Achieving our ambitions is a serious business, but we don't have to be solemn about it. One of the most cheerful clients I ever met was a man in his middle years who had just been wrongfully dismissed from a good job. Far from being depressed, he recounted his story with humour and style, making the rest of the group collapse into fits of laughter. He was not in 'denial' or forcing himself to put on a brave face, but someone who instinctively understood the therapeutic power of laughter. Sadly for the group (but not for him), he was snapped up by the first employer that he approached.

In my work I hear many tales of misunderstandings and general mishaps, mostly concerning interviews. In some people's hands these events become major tragedies, but others see the funny side. One woman finished a particularly impressive presentation to a selection panel, only to glance down and find that she was wearing odd shoes. She told her story with a comic genius that made it impossible to do anything other than laugh.

Another candidate spilled coffee over a furious recruiter's desk, and found himself back on the street within minutes of arrival. He gave a graphic account of his experience, acting out events as if he were performing in a Marx Brothers movie. Neither of these applicants got the job in question, but they refused to let the incidents get them down, and each went on to find what they were looking for soon afterwards.

Rejection and embarrassment are a normal part of life, and you will certainly face your share when climbing the career ladder. Some people have a naturally thick skin, others develop one on the way up. In either case, a healthy sense of the ridiculous is always a great asset. In the meantime, if you are feeling down, one very effective technique for lightening up is to ask yourself: 'Will this really be such a problem in five years' time?'

Progress Check

This has been an intensive course, and it will probably take some time to consolidate all the learning points. Use the checklist below to help you track your progress.

Do I have:

- [ ] regular deep relaxation sessions?
- [ ] a health and fitness plan?
- [ ] a sound knowledge of today's job market?
- [ ] achievable life/career goals?
- [ ] a good idea of how I use my time?
- [ ] an appreciation of positive-thinking techniques?
- [ ] effective self-marketing skills?
- [ ] the know-how to stand up for myself without being offensive?
- [ ] a list of personal and business contacts?
- [ ] a personal career management portfolio?
- [ ] an up-to-date skeleton CV/résumé?

☐ the expertise to mount a structured job-search campaign?
☐ a firm grasp of interview techniques and other selection methods?
☐ the motivation to become a Millennium Candidate?

As we saw at the beginning, this course is about a journey, not just into the 21st century, but into yourself. There can never be a truly accurate prediction of things to come, nor can we ever have total control of external events. However, we *can* take responsibility for our attitude towards change, and it is this that ultimately gives us back our sense of choice. If we have that strong anchor within, then we will never be at the mercy of life's inevitable shocks and tremors.

Of course, the journey is very much a personal one, and no two people will travel exactly the same road. In this, as in everything else, the choice is yours. Use my suggestions or follow a different path. Being a Millennium Candidate does not mean striving for perfection, but simply being open to new ways of doing things. The important thing is to look for *movement*:

From		Towards
stress	→	energy
information	→	knowledge
confusion	→	vision

If you are in doubt about anything, turn back to the course summary, and decide if you need to revisit any of the previous chapters. This book is very much a manual, something that you can come back to whenever the need arises. Some of the techniques and recommendations will become outdated, others will endure, and in time your own knowledge and expertise may well surpass anything you have read here.

At this point, your next big question should be:

> Where do I want to go from here?
> ....
> ....
> ....
> ....
> ....

Once you have the answer, you will be ready to make your own way forward.

And so, the Millennium Master Class has come to an end, but the learning goes on. Whatever you decide to do now, you will never be alone. There are hundreds, even thousands, of people out there waiting to help you. You may not be able to meet them all in person, but they are there anyway, in the pages of books, journals and websites. Learning is there for everyone, whether you are riding high or down on your luck. All you have to do is begin.

SUMMARY

* Planning can be more exciting than implementation, so take action to overcome inertia.
* Once you make a firm commitment to change, things will start to move in your favour.
* Without establishing an inner balance, any outward attempt to reinvent yourself will be superficial and temporary.
* Ways to keep the energy flowing include creative use of colour, Feng Shui and mental workouts.
* Lighten your load by learning to laugh at yourself.

Appendix One
Further Reading

Barger, Nancy J.; Kirby, Linda K; Kummerow, Jean M., *Work Types*: understand your work personality (Warner, US)

Bolles, Richard Nelson, *What Color is Your Parachute?*: a practical manual for job-hunters and career changers (Ten Speed Press, US) Features job-hunting on the Internet and is updated annually.

Barodi, Carol; Levine, John R., *The Internet for Dummies* (IDG Books Worldwide, US)

Buzan, Tony, *Master Your Memory* (BBC Books, UK)

Buzan, Tony, *The Mind Map Book*, (BBC Books, UK)

Jackson, Tom and Ellen, *The Perfect CV*: how to get the job you really want (Piatkus UK/Doubleday US) Contains details of accompanying CV compilation software.

Krause, Donald G., *Sun Tzu: the art of war for executives* (Nicholas Brealey, UK)

Krechowiecka, Irene, *Net That Job!*: using the World Wide Web to develop your career and find work (Kogan Page, UK) An absolute must for anyone wanting a quick, easy guide. Details UK, US and Australian sites.

Oserman, Steve; Riley, Margaret; and Roehm, Frances, *The Guide to Internet Job-Searching* (VGM Career Horizons, US) Probably the most famous of all Internet job-hunting guides.

Pelshenke, Paul, *How to Win at Aptitude Tests* (Thorsons, UK)

Yate, Martin John, *Great Answers to Tough Interview Questions* (Kogan Page, UK/Bob Adams, US)

All of the above books are available in the UK. If Australian or American readers are unable to find any publication that interests them, check whether your local store can order it for you or try an on-line bookstore, such as www.amazon.com (USA and general) or www.amazon.co.uk (UK)

Books published by Element – available in the UK, US and Australia.

Brennan, Richard, *Alexander Technique*
Carrington, Patricia, *Learn to Meditate Kit*
    Includes four audio tapes and step-by-step instruction manual for
    Clinically Standardized Meditation (CSM).
Chiazzari, Suzy, *The Complete Book of Colour*
Doubleday, Tony; Scott, David, *The Elements of Zen*
Heiler, Friedrich, *Prayer*: a study in the history and psychology of
    religion
Mason, Paul, *The Maharishi*
Man-ho Kwok; Palmer, Martin; Ramsay, Jay, *The Illustrated Tao Te*
    Ching
Mortimore, Denise, *Nutritional Healing in a Nutshell*
Purna, Dr Svami, *Balanced Yoga*
Roney-Dougal, Serena, *Where Science and Magic Meet*
Too, Lillian, *Feng Shui Fundamentals – Career*
    One of nine books devoted to specific areas of life to which the art
    can be applied.
Wildwood, Christine, *Aromatherapy: massage with essential oils*
Wong Kiew Kit, *The Complete Book of T'ai Chi Ch'uan*

Appendix Two
Sources of Information

UK – Careers/Job-search Guidance

Career and Outplacement Consultants

Contact the Institute of Personnel and Development for details of consultants who abide by the provisions of the Code of Conduct for Career and Outplacement Consultants. They can also identify 'registered' consultants who have satisfied exacting admission criteria. (See US section below for consultants who have alternatively/additionally received certification from the International Board for Career Management Certification.)

Address: The Careers Adviser
            Institute of Personnel and Development
            IPD House
            Camp Road
            London SW19 4UX
            Tel: 0181 971 9000

Job Centres

High Street Job Centres offer a wide range of free services to job-hunters, including:

➡ nationwide job vacancies
➡ information on training initiatives and other schemes to help people get back to work
➡ basic careers advice
➡ advice and guidance for disabled people and other special communities
➡ referrals to other agencies for advice on careers/state benefits
➡ information on Training and Enterprise Councils and Business Links (see below)

Job Centres are listed in your local telephone directory under 'Employment Service'.

Training and Enterprise Councils (TECs)

Operating around the country, TECs offer training and enterprise schemes through approved suppliers. Many also have careers advice available. Mix of free and fee-paying services, depending on the status of the candidate.

Business Links

'One-stop shops' for those seeking to start up their own business or already running a small company.

Local Careers Services

Services usually free to young people still in full-time education, but adults may have to pay full cost. Provision varies from place to place. Listed in the classified section of the telephone book under 'Careers Guidance Services' (or ask at your local Job Centre).

Useful Internet Sites

Employment Service (Government) Website
http://www.employmentservice.gov.uk/
All the benefits of your local Job Centre on-line, with a Job Kit section that guides you through every aspect of applying for a job. Also explains the Jobseeker's Allowance and the New Deal for young people.

Careers Service Unit Prospects Site
www.prospects.csu.man.ac.uk
Good starting point for graduates, with database of employers which can be searched in a number of ways, depending on your area of interest.

Consultancy Finder
www.fres.co.uk
Allows you to search for recruitment agencies according to sector/function. Also offers job-search tips.

Lifestyle UK
http://lifestyle.co.uk/bh.htm
Just one example of a 'gateway' site that provides links to other sites rather than offering vacancies directly.

Jobsearch – Free CV Posting Service
http://www.jobsearch.co.uk
Creates a standardized page of web information from your input.
This is a site which is likely to be visited by a significant number of
recruiters, but be very cautious about security of personal information. Probably not a good idea to disclose your home or office
address.

Transcendental Meditation

For information on any aspect of TM, including training and scientific research/studies.

Address: Transcendental Meditation
             FREEPOST
             London SW1P 4YY
National enquiry line: 0990 143733
Website: www.transcendental-meditation.org.uk

USA – Careers/Job-search Guidance

Certified Career Management Practitioners and Fellows

The International Board for Career Management Certification holds
a roster of professionals in America and around the world, who have
demonstrated competency in career management and outplacement,
serving as 'advocates for excellence' in their field.

Address: International Board for Career Management
               Certification
             PO Box 150759
             San Rafael
             CA 94915-0759
             USA
             Tel: 415-459-2659
             e-mail: ibcmc@vkam.com

The United States Employment Service (USES)

Nationwide Federal network of local State Employment/Job Service
offices. Offers listings of jobs in your geographical area, plus access
to Interstate Job Bank listings. Some offices also run job-search
workshops.

LifePlan Center

Career, job-search and retirement guidance for the over-fifties. Goal: to create a distinct, richly endowed 'third age' population.

Address: LifePlan Center
5 Third Street
Suite 324
San Francisco
Ca 94103
Tel: 415-546-4499

Useful Internet Sites

America's Job Bank
http://www.ajb.dni.us/
Maintained by Department of Labor, US Employment Service. Links 1,800 state Employment Service offices in the US, listing over 200,000 jobs. Some offices also feature CV databases.

Purdue University Placement Service
http://www.purdue.edu/ups/student/jobsites.htm
This Indiana University site claims to be the Internet's largest link-up service, with over a thousand links to job-searching sites.

Career Path
http://www.careerpath.com/
Lists 'help wanted' ads from over twenty major newspapers in the US.

Handilinks to Employment Agencies
http://www.ahandyguide.com/cat1/e/e126.htm
Lists employment agencies and organizations and career sites for disabled people, veterans and ethnic 'groups'.

The Riley Guide
http://www.dbm.com/jobguide/
Famous gateway site that provides links to other career-related sites. Saves a great deal of search time.

Career Resource Center
http://www.careers.org/index.html
Gateway site listing thousands of links to jobs, employers and careers services.

Transcendental Meditation

For information on any aspect of TM, including training and scientific research/studies.
Tel (toll-free): 1-888-532-7686
Website: http://www.TM.org

Australia – Careers/Job-search Guidance

Career Counsellors

There is currently no national registration or accreditation process, except for psychologists. However, the Australian Association of Career Counsellors is a national organization of practitioners who provide careers services for individuals and organizations' employees to enter into and progress through the world of work. Their objective is to promote the recognition of the professionalism of career counselling through a holistic approach to career and life planning.

Address: The AACC National Office
             PO Box 5084
             Alberton S.A. 5014
             Tel: (08) 8341 1492
             e-mail: aacc@camtech.net.au
             Website: http://www.adelaide.net.au/~aacc

The Centre for Worklife Counselling comprises a network of over thirty professionals providing a range of career development services to individuals and employers in all States of Australia and New Zealand. Their mission extends beyond helping people get the best out of their working hours, by addressing the individual's total needs, including inner well-being, improved relationships and effective performance at work and non-work activities. Its founder/director, Paul Stevens, is the author of twenty-seven publications on worklife and career management issues, including *Stop Postponing the Rest of Your Life* and *A Passion for Work: Our Lifelong Affair*.

Address: The Centre for Worklife Counselling
             PO Box 407
             Spit Junction
             NSW 2088
             Tel: (02) 9968 1588
             Website: http://www.worklife.com.au

Department of Employment, Education, Training and Youth Affairs (DEETYA/DEETYA International Services)

The best way to understand what this government department provides is to visit its Internet site at http://www.deetya.gov.au. Once at its home page you can travel around the DEETYA site to a number of web pages, including the Career Planning Information and Services Directory and details of jobs abroad. The department also produces a number of job-search and career-related products.

Address: Department of Employment, Education, Training and
            Youth Affairs
            16-18 Mort Street
            GPO Box 9880
            Canberra ACT 2601
            Tel: (06) 240 8111

Other Useful Internet Sites

Australian Bureau of Statistics
http://www.abs.gov.au
Labour market information.

Aussie Careers Guide
http://www.northnet.com.au/~achamber
Information about content of occupations with links to personality tests and other useful career sites.

Gradlink
http://www.gradlink.edu.au
Interactive system linking graduates and students with employers.

Job Web Australia
http://www.jobweb.com.au/potajob.htm
Provides job vacancy information and résumé posting service.

Transcendental Meditation

For information on any aspect of TM, including training and scientific research/studies, phone: 613 94674633.

Appendix Three
Internet Sites of Worldwide Interest

The Monster Board
http://www.monster.com
This is the US site, but once in you can connect to the UK or
Australian versions for national vacancies. Also offers 'cyber soci-
eties' for people interested in specific careers, a CV/résumé builder
and a variety of other career-development and job-search tools.

Cool Works
http://www.coolworks.com
Provides links to fascinating jobs and locations, such as American
national parks, cruise ships to Alaska, ski resorts and ranches.
Mostly seasonal work, and non-US residents may require a visa.
Possible that Cool Works will offer an extended service in the future,
including jobs in European locations. One to watch, especially for
the young.

Career Mosaic
http://www.careermosaic.com
Famous American job site, with links to other parts of the world,
including the UK and Australia. Covers all occupational sectors, but
predominance of IT and technical work. In the UK it carries vacancies for several big employers.

AboutWork: Career Database
http://www.aboutwork.com/career/index.html
An American site offering useful guidance for anyone. Includes
scenarios of a range of careers, plus self-assessment exercises and
employment-related chat groups. Also features a résumé quiz which
helps you to choose between style, i.e. chronological, targeted and
functional, then links you to the résumé (CV) maker.

INTEC
http://www.intec.edu.za/career/career.htm
South African college giving free on-line access and scoring of
CareerMatch interest inventory/personality 'test'.

Keirsey Temperament Sorter
http://keirsey.com
Developed by an American clinical psychologist, this world-renowned, free personality test is completed and scored on-line. Also carries lots of useful information on the issues surrounding these types of tests, and gives details of an accompanying book, *Please Understand Me*, which will help you to interpret your results more fully.

On-line Personal Trainer
http://www.fitonline.com
Access to American personal fitness trainers who will design a personal programme for you. Chargeable service.

The above will give you a taste of what's available, but to make the most of the Internet, read up on how to use search engines and directories. Be aware, too, that sites come and go, so it's essential to learn how to surf for alternatives.

Note: All Internet site names are trademarks of their owners.

Index

career portfolio 121–2
career resilience 119–21, 143–4, 210
careers advisors 133–4, 153
careers fairs 131
Chambers of Commerce 105, 136
characteristics, personal 125–6
charitable work 106
childcare 201
China, ancient 75
choice
    career 122–7
    erosion of 6
circulation, staying in 103
clean air 49
Clinically Standardized Meditation (CSM) 28
clothes
    budgeting for 156
    dress code 110, 180
    interview 181–2
clutter 64
college associations 107
colleges 136
colour associations 213–14
'comfort zone' 96–7
communication skills 82–3, 136
company
    events 107
    health policies 49–50
    reports 131
    restructuring 5
complementary techniques, relaxation 27–30
computer
    access to a 156
    literacy 136
    screening 145–6
confidence 93–4, 202
confrontations 76–82
consultants 132–3
contact list 129, 157
contract work 6
constructive criticism 99–100
corporate health policies 49–50
counselling 29–30
counsellors 132
creative awareness 17
credit, giving 96–7
current affairs, awareness of
    at business gatherings 110

at interviews 177
current salary 144
customer service 95–7
CVs (résumés) 210
    advertised vacancies 159
    basic guidelines for 139–41
    at business gatherings 111
    compiling 151–4
    computer screening of 145–6
    disability 145
    examples of 146–51
    format of 141–5
    health details 144
    honesty 140–1
    at interviews 178
    omissions 142–3, 143–4, 144–5
    and speculative approaches 163–4
cyber cafes 114
cycling 43

data skills 125
deadlines 81
decision-making 122–7
deep breathing techniques 111
deep relaxation 169
defeatist attitudes, overcoming 91–3
delay, power of 82
diary entries 63, 110, 113
dieting 46
diffusing difficult situations 78–9
directories 130
disabled people
    adaptive strategies for 202–204
    and CVs 145
    fitness and health of 44–5
    therapies 30
discrimination law 84
distance learning 136
'doing the job' selection process 189
downsizing 6
dress code 110, 180

education 95–6, 142
ego 79
80/20 rule 63
electronic communication overload 61–2

employees, and company restructuring 5–6
employment, leaving reasons 166
employment agencies 153
employment legislation 84
enabling goals 58
engineering 132
entrepreneurs 95–7
environment 48–50
equal opportunities 178
examination results, poor 145
examples of
   advertised vacancy reply letter 159–60
   CVs 146–51
   interview questions 176–7
executive search consultants 103
exercise 41–4
exercises, breathing 25
exhibitions 131
expenses 156

facts, focusing on 78
families 6
fat 46
fax machines 156
fear 8
feedback 97–9, 185
feelgood factor 95, 210
Feng Shui 214–5
finance
   personal budget plan 65–6, 156
   women returners 202
financial global market 3, 5
fitness 37–45, 196, 209
flexible working patterns 6, 38, 120
follow up
   to business gatherings 112–113
   targets 170–71
food guidelines 45
format for CV 141–5
forward planning, for interviews 173–5
fresh air 49

'gain without pain' approach 14, 33
globalization 3, 5
goals
   review 209

setting 54–9
working towards 67
golf 43
government training schemes 107, 136, 199
grades, examination 142, 145
graduates, adaptive strategy 192–5
graphology 189
green, colour association of 213
gyms 107

handwritten letters
   for advertised vacancies 159
   selection process and 189
head-hunters 103
'healing crisis' 32–3
health 38–41, 45–51
   importance of 209
   and older candidates 195–6
health care insurance 50
health clubs 41–2, 107
health details, on CV 144
healthy eating 45–7
higher education 136
holistic approach to well-being 50
home base, for job campaign 155–6
honesty, and CV 140–1
Hong Kong 8
humour 111, 216–17

image, paying attention to 82–3, 97
independent careers consultant 133
influence 72
informal recruitment events 168
information overload 61–2
Information Technology 6, 136, *see also* computers
initiative 194
inner knowledge 9–11
insecurities 7
insomnia 48
Institute of Personnel Development 134
interaction at business gatherings 110–12

interception of negative thoughts 91–3
interests 123, 142
interim management 197
International Association of Career Management Professionals 133
International Board for Career Management Certification 133–4
Internet 42–3, 62, 113–14, 129, 131, 156, 165
interpersonal skills 77–8
interviewers 179, 181
interviews 210
  CVs 178
  forward planning 173–5
  interview day 182–4
  mock 177–82
  negative thoughts 91
  questions 175–7, 179
  rejection 185–6
in-tray selection exercises 188
intuition 14
inward investment
IOU, fitness and health 51–2

Japan 8
job advertisments 153
Job Centres 165
job loss 23
job offers 184–5
job search campaign
  advertised vacancies 157–61
  agencies 164–5
  application forms 166–8
  base for 155–7
  follow up 168–71
  networking 101–15
  recruitment consultants 164–5
  self-promotion 165–6
  speculative approaches 161–4
  targets 168–71
jogging 43

key skills and experience format, CVs 143–4, 147
knowledge, inner 4
Krause, Donald G. 84

laughter 215–16

law 132
layout, CVs 140, 145
leaving employment, reasons for 166
leisure industry 132
letters
  for advertised vacancies 159–63
  'Thank you' 113, 184, 186
libraries 129–31
life expectancy 39
life goals 56–8, 123
life force 13–14
lifelong learning 135–7
lifestyle assessment 40
listening 77–8, 85
logging system 112–13, 121–2, 169–70
logic 14
long term contracts 6
luck, creating own 14, 33

manufacturing 132
marketing 4, 95, 132, 212
martial arts 10, 74–5
maturity 195
medical examinations 39–40
medical profession
  as career 132
  and complementary therapies 30
meditation 27, 30, 31, 75
memory 215
mental preparation 75–6
mergers 8
mind-body techniques 75, 196
Mind Map Book, The 216
mobile phones 64, 95, 182
mock interviews 177–80
months of employment, on CV 145
morale 96
mothers 6, 200–202
motivation 211–17
muscle tension 15, 24
mushin 75

negative thoughts, intercepting 91–3
negotiating 80–2
networking 101–15

THE MILLENNIUM CANDIDATE

prioritizing 59–61
setting goals 54–9
time tracking 63–6
timeless awareness 66–9
trade associations 105–6
trade fairs 131
trade journals 130
training schemes 107, 126, 136, 199
Transcendental Meditation 27
triggers for stress 17–18, 21–2

unemployment
  CVs 143–4
  long term 198–200
universities 107, 136

vibrant stillness 10
vicious circle of stress 19
video link-ups 189
vision, holding onto the 12–13
visualization
  goals 57, 76
  ideal work situation 126–7
  interview outcome 180–1

vocabulary 140, 145–6, 150, 151, 153
voluntary work 106, 137, 178

walking 43
women returners 200–202
work experience 137, 141–2
work processors 140, 156
working from home 64–5
worklists 60
workplace
  goals 58–9
  health and fitness 50–1
  politics 72–4
  'revolution' 5–9
World Wide Web 62
writing-down, importance of
  goals 57
  personal affirmations 92

yellow, colour association of 213
yoga 28, 43
young people, adaptive strategies
  for 192–5

Zen 75